MATT AND

ULTIMATE
FOOTBALL HEROES

MODRIC

FROM THE PLAYGROUND
TO THE PITCH

DINO

Published by Dino Books,
an imprint of John Blake Publishing,
2.25, The Plaza,
535 Kings Road,
Chelsea Harbour,
London SW10 0SZ

www.johnblakepublishing.co.uk

www.facebook.com/johnblakebooks
twitter.com/jblakebooks

First published in paperback in 2018

ISBN: 978 1 78946 096 4

British Library Cataloguing-in-Publication Data:

A catalogue record for this book is available from the British Library.

Design by www.envydesign.co.uk

Printed and bound in Great Britain by Clays Ltd, Elcograf S.p.A.

1 3 5 7 9 10 8 6 4 2

Papers used by John Blake Publishing are natural, recyclable products made from wood grown in sustainable forests. The manufacturing processes conform to the environmental regulations of the country of origin.

Every reasonable effort has been made to trace copyright-holders of material reproduced in this book, but if any have been inadvertently overlooked the publishers would be glad to hear from them.

John Blake Publishing is an imprint of Bonnier Books UK
www.bonnierbooks.co.uk

For all readers,
young and old(er)

Matt Oldfield is an accomplished writer and the editor-in-chief of football review site *Of Pitch & Page*. Tom Oldfield is a freelance sports writer and the author of biographies on Cristiano Ronaldo, Arsène Wenger and Rafael Nadal.

Cover illustration by Dan Leydon.
To learn more about Dan visit danleydon.com
To purchase his artwork visit etsy.com/shop/footynews
Or just follow him on Twitter @danleydon

CONTENTS

CHAPTER 1

CHAMPIONS LEAGUE WINNER

24 May 2014, Estádio da Luz, Lisbon

After nine months of amazing football action, it was time for Europe's biggest match – the Champions League Final!

An incredible 60,000 fans clapped and cheered as the two teams walked out of the tunnel, past the shiny silver trophy, and onto the pitch.

Atleti! Atleti! Atleti!

On one side were Atlético Madrid, wearing their red and white stripes. The new Champions of Spain were a very tough team to beat.

Real! Real! Real!

On the other side were their Madrid rivals, the Galácticos, wearing their blue tracksuit tops. The TV cameras moved along their line of superstars:

Ángel Di María, Gareth Bale, Sami Khedira, Raphaël Varane, Karim Benzema, Cristiano Ronaldo...

Tucked in between these footballing giants was Luka, Real Madrid's little midfield maestro. Luka might not have looked that big, but he was as brave as a lion. Alongside Sami, it would be his job to win the ball and pass it forward to Real's fantastic forwards.

'This is our year, lads!' Real's captain Iker Casillas called out before kick-off. 'Let's win *La Décima*!'

The Real Madrid fans had been waiting twelve long years to win their tenth Champions League title. They were getting desperate! But after losing in the semi-finals for three years in a row, their team had, at last, made it all the way to the final once again. Now, they just had to win it.

From the very first minute, Luka controlled the game calmly for Real. It was his first-ever Champions

League final but it didn't look that way. What a natural!

Control, turn, perfect pass,
Control, turn, perfect pass,
Control, turn, dribble, then perfect pass!

Luka was always looking to create a goalscoring chance but he never rushed his pass. Patience was key. Eventually, a gap would appear in the Atlético defence.

At 5 feet 8 inches, Luka was one of the smallest players on the pitch, but what did size matter with so much spirit? He made tackles, intercepted passes, and he even won headers!

In the thirty-sixth minute, however, Atlético took the lead. Luka could only watch as Diego Godín's header looped up over Iker's outstretched arm. *1–0!*

'Keep going!' the Real centre-back Sergio Ramos urged his teammates. 'We've got plenty of time to grab an equaliser.'

Luka wasn't the kind of player to panic. He just kept doing what he always did, pushing Real Madrid up the pitch.

Control, turn, perfect pass,
Control, turn, perfect pass,
Control, turn, dribble, then perfect pass!

But as the second half flew by, Real still hadn't scored. Thibaut Courtois saved Cristiano's free kick. Karim shot wide, then Isco, then Gareth.

'How many chances do we need?' Luka groaned, reading the minds of all the anxious Real Madrid supporters in the stands.

When he raced over to take a corner, the match was deep into injury time. It was now or never in the Champions League final...

Luka curled a beautiful cross towards the penalty spot and hoped for the best. There was lots of pushing and shoving in the box but suddenly, Sergio sprang up and headed the ball into the net. *1–1!*

Over by the corner flag, Luka threw his arms up triumphantly. 'We did it!' he roared.

What a goal, and what a time to score it! The Atlético players were distraught; the Real players were delighted. Their *Décima* dream was still alive.

In extra time, Real raced away to victory. Ángel's

shot was saved, but Gareth was in the right place to score the rebound. *2–1!*

'Yes!' Luka screamed as he celebrated with his old Tottenham teammate.

This was why they had both moved to Real Madrid – for the glory, for the trophies. When it came to winning, the team was totally ruthless.

Marcelo dribbled forward and shot past Courtois. *3–1!*

Cristiano scored from the penalty spot. *4–1!*

Luka bounced up and down with his brilliant teammates in front of the Real Madrid fans. They were the new Champions of Europe!

After a bad start, it had turned out to be the best night of Luka's life by far. He had a Croatian flag wrapped around his shoulders, a winners' medal around his neck, and soon, he would have the Champions League trophy in his hands!

But first, it was Iker's turn. As the Real Madrid captain lifted the cup high above his head, clouds of white confetti filled the sky. It was time to get the party started.

Campeones, Campeones, Olé! Olé! Olé!

When the trophy finally reached Luka, he held on tightly. Wow, it was huge, and quite heavy too. Imagine if he dropped it!

'Hurray!' he yelled up into the Lisbon night sky.

It was a moment that Luka would treasure forever. He was a football superstar now. He knew that his grandad would be so proud of him.

CHAPTER 2

GOAT HERDING WITH GRANDAD

'Luka!' a tired voice shouted through the open back door. 'Where are you? I need your help please. We've got work to do.'

'Coming, Grandad!' Luka replied, remembering to grab his coat off the hook before he rushed outside. In winter, it could be bitterly cold on the slopes of the Velebit mountain range where the Modrić family lived.

'Good boy,' his Grandad said, giving him a hearty pat on the back. 'Right, let's go.'

As Luka walked beside his grandad, he didn't look up at the wild, lonely landscape that surrounded them. He was used to those views. It was his home, after all. Instead, he kept his head down, looking at the path ahead. He did this for two reasons. The first reason was that the ground was rocky and uneven, and he didn't want to trip and fall. The second reason was that he was searching for the perfect stick.

Luka couldn't herd goats without a good stick – no way! That would be like asking a footballer to play without a football.

'Not bad,' his grandad nodded approvingly when Luka showed him the stick he had chosen. 'That will do nicely.'

Luka was still only five years old but that was old enough to go goat herding with his grandad. Besides, if he didn't help out, who else could? There weren't any kind neighbours nearby; their house was the only house on the street. And Luka's parents, Stipe and Radojka, were too busy working long hours in a local knitwear factory in order to earn money for the family.

So, goat herding was Luka's job and he took it very

seriously. That's why picking the perfect stick was so important.

'No, wrong way!' Luka told any goats that tried to take a different route. He was still very small but he was brave enough to block their path. 'That's it – follow your brothers and sisters!'

It was so peaceful up on the mountain paths. Most of the time, it was just Luka, the goats, and Grandad. What in the world could be better than that? There weren't many other young children in the area, so Grandad was his best friend. As they walked, the old man told lots of exciting stories about his life, and Luka listened carefully, taking in every word.

'But now, the times are changing,' his grandad often warned on their goat-herding adventures together. 'Trouble is on its way.'

Unfortunately, Luka's grandad turned out to be right about that. First came war and sorrow, and then came football and joy.

CHAPTER 3

THE SORROWS
OF WAR

On a cold December day in 1991, just a week
before Christmas, Luka's grandad led the goats along
the mountain slopes as usual. This time, however,
he was alone because Luka was busy learning at
school. And, sadly, their homeland was no longer
a peaceful place.

Their country, Croatia, was fighting fiercely to
become an independent nation, separate from
Yugoslavia. Yugoslavia, however, weren't going to let
them leave without a fight. On that cold December
day, soldiers suddenly stormed the village of Modrići,
and Luka's grandad was killed.

When he returned from school and heard the

tragic news, Luka was absolutely devastated. He loved his grandad so much and now they would never be able to goat herd together again. How could such a horrible thing happen to his poor, innocent grandad? War was a very difficult thing for a six-year-old child to understand.

'I'm so sorry, Luka,' his mum told him tearfully, 'but we have to leave this place straight away. It's not safe to stay here any longer.'

Their happy days in Modrići were over; now, they were refugees on the run. The family quickly packed up their belongings and moved to Zadar, the nearest city, where Luka and his sister Jasmina had been born.

What now? They had nowhere to live, and they didn't have enough money to rent a new house of their own. Fortunately, they were offered a small, bare room in the Hotel Kolovare. They didn't have electricity or running water, but at least they had a shelter from the war.

But even in Zadar, things were far from safe. All through the day and through the night, Luka and his family lived with the loud sounds of war. Even

walking out into the streets was a dangerous thing
to do. As the fight for independence went on, there
was more and more damage everywhere. They were
tough and terrible times for the Croatian nation.

'One day, everything will be peaceful again,'
Luka's mum promised them as they huddled together
to keep warm.

But when? Luka wanted to go back to Modrići.
In Zadar, he was only an hour's drive from his old
home, but it felt like a lifetime away. It was such
a shock to go from the quiet of the countryside to
the noise and bustle of a city. Compared to Modrići,
Zadar felt really big and scary. There were strange,
sad faces everywhere he looked.

'Dad, when are we going back home?' Luka asked
again and again.

'We can't, son,' Stipe always replied, his face full of
sorrow. 'This is our home now.'

Luka never stopped missing Modrići, the
mountains, the goats and most of all, his grandad.
But luckily, he found a new love that helped him to
escape from the sorrows of war...

CHAPTER 4

THE JOYS OF FOOTBALL

Nothing could ever replace his beloved grandad, but during those years living at the Hotel Kolovare, Luka discovered a new best friend – a small, battered old football. With that ball at his feet, he turned out to be a natural.

Every day, when the grenades stopped firing and the ground stopped shaking, Luka would rush out the door with the ball tucked under his arm.

'Son, where are you going?' his mum would ask worriedly as he dropped the ball and dribbled his way out of their room and down the halls of the hotel. He always ran as fast as he could, dodging past any obstacles in his way.

'I'm just going outside!' he replied over his shoulder.

'Okay, but stay safe,' his mum warned. 'And if you hear any more grenades, run to the shelter right away!'

By 'outside', Luka meant the hotel car park. It still wasn't safe to play football in the streets of Zadar, but at least he had that small square of concrete. That was as far as he was allowed to go, and so that became his football pitch. Every day, no matter the weather, he went out there to practise his skills. What else was there to do?

At first, Luka would just play by himself, bouncing the ball against the hotel's walls:

Right foot control, right foot pass!

Left foot control, left foot pass!

Right foot control, turn, dribble, right foot shot!

Left foot control, left foot shot!

When he was really in the zone, Luka found that he forgot all about the war and sorrow that surrounded him. With a ball at his feet, he could ignore the smoke that filled the sky, and escape to a world of fun and football.

Most of the time, the workers at the Hotel Kolovare were happy to see a young boy getting some exercise and having a good time. Sometimes, they even stopped to join in.

'Over here, Luka,' they called out. 'Pass!'

'Wow, you're getting good at this!' they encouraged him.

As Luka got better and better at football, so did the accuracy of his passing and shooting. Soon, he could aim high or low, left or right, and always hit his target.

It was all fun and games, just as long as Luka didn't do any damage. However, sometimes, he just couldn't help himself. With each challenge he completed, he set himself a new, harder one. He always achieved his aims, but occasionally he left broken glass along the way.

'Sorry!' he shouted each time a ball smashed through a window.

'Hey!' a voice shouted back.

Oh dear, would they be angry at him? Would they take his ball away? Luka put on his best innocent face and went inside to beg for forgiveness.

'Sorry, it won't happen again. I'll be more careful, I promise!'

It worked every time. After a few mumbles and grumbles, he always got his beloved ball back. The hotel workers couldn't bear to take away the joy of football.

'Thanks!'

The car park wasn't big enough for proper football matches but sometimes there was enough room for Luka to have a kickaround with a few friends. There were lots of families staying at the Hotel Kolovare, and that meant lots of bored young kids.

'Come on, let's PLAY!' Luka led the way outside. He was their Pied Piper of Hamelin, holding his beloved ball above his head like a trophy.

Luka was small and skinny for his age but he was a lot tougher than he looked. All the bad things that had happened to him – losing his grandad, leaving Modrići – had only made him stronger. When it came to football, Luka was determined to be the best. Even playing two-on-two in the Kolovare car park, he had to win.

'Right, our turn to start,' he said, grabbing the ball and placing it down at his feet. Luka and his best friend Marko were losing 2–1 against Ivan and Nikola.

'Pass it now!' Marko shouted, waving his arms in the air, but Nikola was there waiting to block it. So, Luka faked to pass and played it through Ivan's legs instead.

NUTMEG!

Nikola raced over to make a tackle but Luka skipped straight past him like he was a suitcase in the halls of the hotel.

Olé!

Luka was through – he just needed to tap the ball gently against the wall to score. But in his head, he wasn't there in the car park anymore; he was playing on a proper pitch in front of thousands of cheering fans and a big goalkeeper was charging out towards him.

Luka pulled back his right leg and kicked the ball with all his power. *BANG!*

*Gooooooooooooooooooooaaaaaaaaaaaaaaaalllllllllllll
llllllllllllll!!!!!!!!!!!!!!!!!!!!*

The wonderstrike flew through the air like an arrow
and… *SMASH!* through another hotel window.

'Sorry!'

Uh oh, it was definitely time for Luka to find a
bigger space to show off his super football skills.

CHAPTER 5

ZADAR

'The kid who kicks a ball around in the hotel car park' – that's what Josip Bajlo called Luka at first.

Bajlo was the chairman of the best local club, NK Zadar, and he was always looking out for top young talent. One day, he got an interesting phone call from a worker at the Hotel Kolovare. Apparently, they had a future superstar playing in their car park!

When Bajlo went there to scout the boy, he wasn't disappointed. Luka's super football skills caught his eye immediately.

'The kid is small and skinny,' Bajlo explained to his youth coaches, 'but trust me, with the ball at his feet, he's a very special player.'

The Zadar chairman looked around at the faces in the room. No, they didn't seem very interested. The coaches had probably stopped listening as soon as he said 'small and skinny'. Croatia prided itself on its strong, powerful footballers.

'Fine, if you don't believe me, go check him out for yourselves,' Bajlo continued. 'He's there practising in the car park, all day every day. When you get there, you'll know who I'm talking about. Just look for the boy with the golden touch.'

One look and the coaches changed their minds completely.

'Wow, that kid can really *play!*'

'Look at that touch! He could be just what we need here at Zadar – something different.'

Soon, Luka got an invitation to his first ever football training session. How exciting! He didn't know what to expect but he wasn't nervous. No way, what was there to be nervous about? He was off to play football – his favourite thing in the world – on a proper grass pitch.

'I can't wait for this!' Luka told his dad on the way

to the training pitch. It was too dangerous for him to walk there on his own during wartime.

'Just make sure you enjoy yourself, okay?' Stipe replied. 'I believe in you, son!'

They still couldn't afford to move out of the Hotel Kolovare, but Luka's parents had saved up enough money to buy their son his own pair of football boots and some shin pads too.

'You're going to need those against the bigger boys!' Radojka said protectively.

'Wow, cool!' Luka replied, staring in wonder at the shin pads in his hands. Not only did they have a big 'Nike' tick on them, but they also had a picture of Brazil's star striker, Ronaldo. 'These are the best ever. Thanks, Mum! Thanks, Dad!'

Wearing his shiny new shin pads, Luka felt eight feet tall and full of confidence. That was a good thing because when he arrived at the training pitch, he was easily the smallest and skinniest kid there. Some of the Zadar players towered over him like tall buildings.

Gulp, they were going to eat Luka alive! Was it too

late to change his mind and go back to kicking a ball around in the car park? No, he had to be brave.

'Good luck!' Stipe said, pushing him forward.

'Right, we've got a new player joining us today,' the Zadar youth coach announced before the session began, putting an arm on his shoulder. 'Everybody, this is Luka. Please make him feel welcome!'

Luka smiled nervously, hoping that his pounding heart wouldn't burst right out of his chest. He thought about his dad's words – 'I believe in you, son!' – and he thought about his beloved grandad. As he remembered their adventures together, he could feel himself growing stronger and stronger like a superhero. It was time for Luka to prove himself and make them proud.

Luka aced the passing drills, no problem. After all, he had spent months – no, *years* – practising in the car park. Plus, he was the boy with the golden touch.

Right foot control, right foot pass!

Left foot control, left foot pass!

'Excellent control, Luka!' one of the youth coaches clapped.

Phew! He was off to a good start, but eventually, Luka knew that he would have to face Zadar's big, tough tacklers.

'Bring it on!' they grinned at him, licking their lips like evil monsters.

The first time the ball came to him, Luka took a touch and then looked up for a teammate and... *CRUNCH*!

His opponent won the tackle and left Luka lying sprawled out on the grass. *Owwwww*! It felt like he had been tackled by a train, not an eight-year-old human being!

But Luka didn't complain. He picked himself back up and carried on playing. To make sure that he didn't let that happen again, he had two main options:

1) Think faster and pick out a killer pass straight away, OR

2) Use his dribbling skills to skip past the tough tackle.

Luka knew that he was good enough to do either, or even both at the same time! He was going to show the Zadar coaches that the biggest kids weren't always the best players.

'Pass it!' Luka called out in the middle of the pitch. He had one eye on the ball as it rolled towards him, and one eye on the tacklers that were coming towards him. He knew what to do next.

Right foot control, turn and...

Luka flicked the ball cleverly around the first challenge and chased after it...

Olé!

Luka ran forward until a big defender blocked his path. He faked to go left but went right instead...

Olé!

Okay, what next? Luka shielded the ball brilliantly until he spotted his teammate's run. *PING –* PERFECT PASS!

Goooooooooooooooooooooaaaaaaaaaaaaaaaaalllllllllllll llllllllllllll!!!!!!!!!!!!!!!!!!!

'That was amazing!' the goalscorer cheered, giving Luka a friendly hug. 'I'm Mario, by the way.'

Soon, Luka and Mario were a deadly double act, tearing teams apart with their speed and skill. Even

Hajduk Split, the most famous team in Croatia, couldn't handle them.

As Bajlo watched his Under-11s team win, he couldn't help beaming with pride. What a brilliant decision! He had been right about Luka; he was proving to be a very special player indeed.

But the Zadar chairman wasn't the only one watching that match. The Hajduk youth coaches were very impressed by two players in particular.

'The little guy in midfield is very good,' they decided, 'but the bigger boy up front is even better. That's a top talent, right there!'

Hajduk offered Mario a two-week trial, but what about Luka? No, he would be staying at Zadar... for now.

'Don't worry, you'll be joining me at Hajduk in no time!' Mario reassured him.

CHAPTER 6

HAJDUK HEARTBREAK

Luka couldn't help feeling a little disappointed but he didn't give up on his dream. He kept working hard at Zadar and six months later, Hajduk Split offered him a two-week trial too.

'It'll be the Luka and Mario Show all over again!' Luka told his friend excitedly.

Together, they looked ahead to an awesome football future where they were the superstars of the Hajduk first team.

'And Croatia too!' Mario decided.

Luka couldn't wait for his trial to begin. After all, Hajduk were his favourite team in the world. Okay, so they didn't have anyone like Ronaldo, but they had lots of top national team players like Aljoša Asanović and Igor Štimac. And they had won the Croatian First Football League title for the last two years in a row.

As his big day approached, Luka imagined lifting the shiny league trophy at the Poljud stadium in front of thousands of fans, chanting:

We love you, Luka!

Modrić! Modrić! Modrić!

'No wait,' Luka stopped himself, 'one step at a time!'

It was good to dream big but he was only ten years old. He had a long way to go and he couldn't get carried away just yet. First, he had to impress the Hajduk youth coaches, and that wouldn't be easy at all.

'Yes, the dream team is back together!' Mario cheered, giving Luka a big hug as he arrived at the Hajduk training ground.

He was glad to see at least one familiar face. Otherwise, it was like his first day at Zadar all over again – little Luka in a group of giants. And this time, not only were the other players really big, but they were also really, really good at football.

'How on earth am I going to compete against *them*?' Luka panicked.

No, he couldn't think like that. He was stronger than he looked and besides, he had a super power: his golden touch. He could do this! Luka thought about his dad's words – 'I believe in you, son!' – and he thought about his beloved grandad. As he remembered their adventures together, he could feel himself growing stronger and stronger like a superhero.

Luka had proved himself at Zadar, and now he was going to prove himself at Hajduk. This was a big step-up, but he was ready to shine. He just needed to keep doing what he did at Zadar every week.

Control, turn, perfect pass,
Control, turn, perfect pass.

'That's it – well done, Luka!' the coaches clapped.

His confidence grew with every kick, and his fears faded away. He was playing football, his favourite thing in the world.

Luka started off playing simple passes but he soon moved on to more complicated stuff. After all, he had to stand out from the crowd.

As a playmaker, he needed to create clever chances for the strikers, and maybe even score a few goals of his own. When he spotted some space ahead of him, he went for it:

Control, turn, dribble, SHOOT!

Goooooooooooooooooooaaaaaaaaaaaaaaaaallllllllllll llllllllllllll!!!!!!!!!!!!!!!!!!!!

Luka enjoyed his time at Hajduk so much that he forgot that it was only a trial. Before he knew it, the two weeks were over, and he and his dad were sitting in the youth team director's office.

'Luka has really impressed everyone with his attitude and talent,' the director began positively. Sadly, however, that praise was followed by a 'but'.

'But I'm afraid that his size is a problem. It's not just his height; it's also his strength. I'm sorry, we just don't think that he's ready to play for this club.'

Sitting there in his chair, Luka's heart sank towards the floor. How could his Hajduk dream be over already? As he left the room, he was too heartbroken to say a single word. It was only on the journey home that he broke his silence.

'I don't understand – the coaches said I was playing well!' he wailed. 'I worked hard, I didn't give the ball away, and I was brave against the big boys. I can't help being small! What did I do wrong?'

'Absolutely nothing,' his dad said, trying his best to comfort him. 'I know it's not fair, son, but you'll get another chance, I promise. If not at Hajduk, then somewhere else! This isn't the end of your football journey; it's just the beginning.'

But where to now – back to Zadar? He loved playing for his local team but there were two problems with that plan.

Firstly, Luka hadn't told the head of the youth academy, Tomislav Bašić, about the Hajduk trial.

Secondly, Tomislav had found out anyway, and he was furious.

In fact, he was so furious that when Luka turned up at training, his coach just shook his head. 'Sorry, if you're not good enough to play for Hajduk, then you're not good enough to play for Zadar either.'

Luka was devastated. His big football dream had turned into a total nightmare!

'If I don't have a team to play for, what's the point of playing at all?' he asked himself one day. He still kicked a ball around in the hotel car park on his own, but it just wasn't the same.

Thankfully, just when Luka was seriously thinking about quitting football altogether, Tomislav went to speak to Stipe. Luka's suffering was over.

'Your son has learnt his lesson now,' the coach decided. 'It's time for him to return to Zadar. We need him!'

When his dad told him the good news, Luka felt so relieved. *Phew!* He made up his mind straight away – no, he wasn't ready to give up on his big football dream yet. It was his favourite thing in the world and he couldn't wait to start playing again.

'I'm back, and I'm going to be better than ever!' he assured his coach at training.

Tomislav nodded and smiled, 'That's it, Luka – don't listen to Hajduk. They don't know what they're talking about! I believe in you, kid. You've got what it takes to become a top footballer – the talent *and* the toughness. And if you'll let me, I'm going to help you get there.'

CHAPTER 7

EURO 96

While Luka and Tomislav were working together on the Zadar training field, the Croatia national team was setting off for England to play at Euro 96. The whole nation was so excited because it was going to be their first football tournament as an independent country. How would they get on against top teams like Germany, France and England?

'No problem, we can beat anyone!' the Croatian people boasted proudly.

Luka couldn't agree more. He was full of hope as the competition kicked off. He couldn't wait to see his national team in action on TV, wearing their red-and-white chequered shirts, and making history.

'We're going all the way!' Luka told everyone at the Hotel Kolovare. He said it so confidently, as if it was a fact rather than an opinion. 'Boban will lead us to glory!'

Zvonimir Boban was Croatia's captain and midfield playmaker, and therefore, Luka's ultimate football hero. No, he didn't have Boban's height (yet!), but with Tomislav's help, he was developing the passing range and dribbling skills to rival his hero.

'Soon, that's going to be me!' Luka promised himself as the 'Chequered Ones' took the field against Turkey.

He was still only eleven years old but after his Hajduk heartbreak, Luka was feeling more determined than ever. As his dad had told him, his football journey was only just beginning. One day, he would become his country's greatest player but while Euro 96 was going on, he focused on being his country's biggest fan.

'Come on, Croatia!' Luka cheered loudly.

Eighty-five anxious minutes later, however, the score was still 0–0.

'Come on, Croatia!' Luka carried on cheering

loudly. They needed his support more than ever.

One second, Croatia were defending a corner and the next, they were on the counter-attack! Aljoša Asanović passed to Goran Vlaović, who burst into the Turkey half.

'Go on, Goran!' Luka yelled at the TV screen.

On the edge of the penalty area, Vlaović dribbled around the goalkeeper and slid the ball into the empty net. 1–0!

Croatia! Croatia! Croatia!

When the final whistle blew, the whole nation celebrated like the trophy was theirs.

'I knew we'd win!' Luka said with a big smile.

Thankfully, the next game against Denmark wasn't as tight and tense. In the second half, Davor Šuker threaded a great pass through to Mario Stanić, who tried to dribble around Peter Schmeichel...

'PENALTY!' Luka cried out as Stanić tumbled to the ground.

The referee pointed to the spot and Šuker stepped up... and scored. 1–0!

But Luka knew that the match wasn't over yet.

'Come on, Croatia!' he carried on cheering loudly.

Half an hour later, Šuker crossed from the left and there was Luka's hero Boban, sliding in at the back post. 2–0!

Croatia! Croatia! Croatia!

Boban stood in front of his fans, pumping both his fists passionately. The team captain's celebration was one that Luka would copy many times out in the hotel car park. That, and Šuker's cheeky chip to make it 3–0.

Croatia! Croatia! Croatia!

Luka and his country were having the time of their lives. Even a 3–0 defeat to Portugal in their next game couldn't dampen their spirits. In their first-ever tournament, Croatia were through to the quarter-finals of Euro 96!

'I told you!' Luka reminded everyone at the Hotel Kolovare. 'We're going all the way!'

First, however, Croatia would have to get past one of the giants of European football – Germany. They had Matthias Sammer at the back, Andreas Möller in midfield, and Jürgen Klinsmann in attack.

'Yes, but we've got Bilić, Boban and Šuker!' Luka argued proudly.

As the Croatian team walked out on to the pitch at Old Trafford, Luka felt the most nervous he'd ever felt in his young life. *Playing* football was a lot easier than watching it.

Croatia! Croatia! Croatia!

In the twentieth minute, Sammer dribbled into the penalty area, past Nikola Jerkan...

'Handball!' cried Germany.

'No way, that was accidental!' cried Croatia.

But again, the referee pointed to the penalty spot. Klinsmann stepped up and scored. 1–0 to Germany!

'Come on, Croatia!' Luka cheered louder than ever.

Early in the second half, Nikola Jurčević rushed forward to steal the ball off Steffen Freund. He passed to super Šuker, who wasn't going to miss. 1–1!

Croatia! Croatia! Croatia!

In Zadar, Luka jumped for joy. They were back in the game! Unfortunately, it all went wrong after that. First, defender Igor Štimac was sent off, and then three minutes later, Sammer scored to make it 2–1 to Germany.

Despite all of Luka's support, Croatia just couldn't equalise again. They were out of Euro 96, but they had battled so bravely. The players clapped the fans, who clapped right back. They were all very disappointed but also very proud of everything they had achieved. Croatia were now on the football map!

Luka wiped away his tears and rushed outside to practise his skills. He had lots of work to do! As he ran, Luka did some important maths in his head:

At World Cup 1998, he would be… thirteen – impossible!

At Euro 2000, he would be… fifteen – still impossible!

At World Cup 2002, he would be… seventeen – just about possible!

At Euro 2004, he would be… nineteen – definitely possible!

That 2004 tournament became his big new target. By then, with Tomislav by his side, Luka would surely be 'the next Boban', leading Croatia to football glory.

CHAPTER 8

DREAMS COME TRUE AT DINAMO

The 1998 World Cup made Luka even more determined to play for his country. Bilić, Boban and Šuker were all back, and the team looked better than ever.

Jamaica 1 Croatia 3!

Japan 0 Croatia 1!

Romania 0 Croatia 1!

Luka watched every game in Zadar with his friends and family. With each win, the nation grew happier and happier.

'Imagine if we won the World Cup!' Luka's dad joked. 'The party would go on for weeks!'

Suddenly, the impossible seemed possible. In the

quarter-finals, Croatia beat their Euro 96 enemies, Germany, 3–0. They were through to the World Cup semi-finals for the first time ever!

'We're going all the way!' Luka told everyone at the Hotel Kolovare again, and this time, many of them believed him.

When Croatia lost 2–1 to France, Luka was distraught. He cried and cried at the final whistle, but three days later, his sorrow turned to joy. Šuker scored the winner as Croatia beat the Netherlands in the third-place play-off.

Third place in the World Cup – that was basically a bronze medal! It was the greatest success in Croatian football history.

'For now!' Luka kept telling himself. 'Just you wait until I become the next Boban!'

His long hours of hard work with Tomislav didn't pay off straight away, however. Instead, he carried on starring for the Zadar Under-13s,

then the Under-14s,

then the Under-15s...

'When are the big clubs going to notice me?' Luka

asked, looking very dejected.

'Be patient,' Tomislav told him again and again, 'and keep growing!'

Unfortunately, size was still Luka's biggest issue. Despite his increasing talent and toughness, the scouts just took one look at the small, skinny kid and thought, 'No way, he can't battle with the big boys!'

Luka was doing everything he could to grow bigger and stronger. He ate as much food as he could find, and then completed Tomislav's challenging fitness drills. He even spent hours hanging from the crossbar by his arms.

'Maybe this will help to stretch me out!' Luka hoped.

Slowly, he was growing taller and taller, but he was never going to be a giant. A club would have to accept him as he was, and take a chance on the boy with the golden touch.

That club turned out to be Hajduk Split's big rivals, Dinamo Zagreb. After an impressive youth tournament in Italy, Tomislav arranged for his young star to go on trial at Dinamo.

'You're the best!' Luka thanked his coach excitedly. 'This time, I'm not taking "no" for an answer!'

Arriving at the Dinamo training ground, Luka was pumped up and ready to perform. This was it – his big opportunity to make it as a professional footballer. Despite his dad's kind words, this might be his last chance. Sadly, clubs in Croatia weren't crying out for little playmakers. He had to find a way to stand out from the crowd.

'I can do this,' Luka told himself. He owed it to himself, to Tomislav, and most of all to his family. They had moved to another, slightly nicer hotel in Zadar, but they still didn't have a home of their own. That was because they were spending most of their money on helping Luka to achieve his football dream. They were counting on him; he couldn't let them down…

…And he didn't. At the trial, Luka left the Dinamo coaches spellbound. They had a new maestro in the middle! He controlled the game with his two magic wands:

Right foot control, turn, right foot pass!

Left foot control, turn, left foot pass!

Luka made football look so simple, and so beautiful.

Control, turn, perfect pass,

Control, turn, perfect pass.

And if he spotted some space ahead of him:

Control, turn, dribble, SHOOT!

Luka set up goals and Luka scored goals, too. Size didn't matter when you had that much talent and toughness.

'We *have* to sign him!' the Dinamo coaches decided straight away.

At the age of fifteen, Luka's football dream had finally come true. By joining the Dinamo academy, he was following in the footsteps of Croatia's Euro 96 stars like Robert Prosinečki, Davor Šuker, and his number one hero, Zvonimir Boban.

'I owe you big time!' Luka thanked his coach. 'I really couldn't have done this without you.'

'No, you earned your place here,' Tomislav told him. 'You worked so hard for this and you never gave up. Now, go become the new Boban, or even better!'

That was Luka's big plan. Now that he was a Dinamo player, there would be no stopping him. Hajduk Split, beware!

'Congratulations,' Luka's parents cheered proudly when he shared the great news. 'We knew you could do it!'

One day, when he signed his first big professional contract, Luka would buy them a beautiful home of their own. What an emotional day that would be for all of them!

But Luka couldn't relax and get too comfortable just yet...

CHAPTER 9

LEARNING ON LOAN

Luka's first year at Dinamo soon flew by, full of ups and downs. He was playing regularly for the youth team, but he struggled to be their midfield maestro in every match.

At Zadar, it had been easy to stand out but at Dinamo, he was just one of many promising young playmakers. The pressure was on to perform. The problem was that sometimes, Luka was magical, but at other times, he was muscled off the ball.

'Come on, you've got to be stronger there!' Romeo Jozak shouted at him.

The Dinamo youth coach was asking himself the same old questions about Luka. He had no

doubt about the boy's technical skills, but would
he be tough enough to handle the physicality of
professional football? He had the football brain, but
did he have the football *heart*?

The answer, of course, was yes, but Luka needed
to prove it. So, ahead of the 2003–04 season, he was
called in to see the Dinamo youth coach. Uh oh!
Was it happening again? Were the club asking him to
leave already? Luka was really panicking by the time
he knocked and then entered.

'We're sending you out on loan to Zrinjski Mostar,'
Jozak informed him.

Luka was glad to hear that he wasn't leaving
Dinamo for good, but his heart was still pounding
in his chest. Zrinjski were a team in the Bosnian
League, which was famous for being one of the
toughest and roughest in the whole of Europe. Luka
was still a small, skinny eighteen-year-old. If he
wasn't careful, they would eat him alive!

'No, I can't think like that,' he stopped himself.
'I'll just have to be even braver than ever!'

Luka thought back to his early days at Zadar. After

a few crunching tackles, he had learnt to be clever with the ball. If he acted fast, they couldn't catch him. It was time for him to prove once again that the biggest kids weren't always the best players.

'Welcome,' the Zrinjski manager Stjepan Deverić said, giving him a firm handshake. He looked Luka up and down, from his little legs to his baby face, and then added, 'I hope you're ready for a real battle!'

Luka just nodded determinedly. He'd let his golden touch do the talking.

Control, turn, perfect pass,
Control, turn, perfect pass...

Deverić was impressed with his new playmaker straight away. For a small kid, he had a huge heart.

'Yes, he's got the strength to succeed,' the manager decided.

Before long, Luka was in the Zrinjski starting line-up and once he got there, he stayed there. His learning curve was steep on Bosnia's rock-hard pitches, but he always picked himself up and played on, no matter what. It was all part of his football journey.

Mostly, Luka created chances for his teammates, but if he spotted some space, he went for goal.

Control, turn, dribble, SHOOT!

In his twenty-two games for Zrinjski, Luka scored eight goals and set up lots more. They didn't win the league but Luka went home to Croatia with the Player of the Year award. Not bad for a small, skinny eighteen-year-old.

'So, how was it?' his Dinamo teammates asked him at training. 'We weren't sure that you'd make it back alive!'

Luka laughed. 'Put it this way – if you can play in the Bosnian League, you can play anywhere!'

His adventures weren't over yet, though. The next year, Luka was off again but this time, he stayed in Croatia. Dinamo decided to loan three of their youngsters – Luka and defenders Vedran Ćorluka and Hrvoje Čale – to their local neighbours, NK Inter Zaprešić. It was a great way for them to gain more first-team experience.

'Welcome,' their manager Srećko Bogdan said, giving Luka another firm handshake. Bogdan looked him up and down, from his little legs to his baby face, and warned, 'This won't be a walk in the park. You'll have to earn your place here.'

Luka just nodded determinedly. He'd let his golden touch do the talking once again.

It only took Luka a month to earn his place as Zaprešić's star playmaker. Playing behind the strikers, he had the freedom to create as much magic as possible. He dribbled past defenders, always on the look-out for the perfect path to...

Gooooooooooooooooooooaaaaaaaaaaaaaaaaalllllllllllll llllllllllllll!!!!!!!!!!!!!!!!!!!

'You've got to stop the little guy!' opposition managers shouted angrily. 'He's running rings around you!'

Yes, sometimes Luka still got pushed around, but most of the time, he had the speed, the skill and the intelligence to escape with the ball.

'Wow, how did he even do that?' Bogdan often marvelled.

Playing week in week out, Luka was getting better and better, and so was his team. It was

only Zaprešić's second season in the Croatian First
League but suddenly, thanks to their mini midfield
maestro, they found themselves in the race for
the title! Dinamo, meanwhile, were way down in
mid-table.

'They made a big mistake letting us go out on
loan!' Vedran joked.

In the end, Zaprešić finished second, two
points behind Luka's old enemies, Hajduk. It was
an amazing achievement for the club, and their
highest-ever league position. Not only that, but
Zaprešić had qualified for the first round of the
UEFA Cup.

'We'll be playing in Europe next season!' their
players cheered joyfully.

Luka was there at the centre of the team
celebrations. What a season it had been for him!
Suddenly, everyone was talking about his talent. He
won the league's Hope of the Year award for best
young player and he also received his first call-up to
the Croatia Under-21 squad.

Wow, everything was clicking neatly into place.

So, what next? One thing was for sure: Zaprešić would be heading off on their European adventures without their mini midfield maestro.

During his two loan spells away, Luka had really proved himself. It was time for him to return to Dinamo and become their new Number 10.

CHAPTER 10

GLORY DAYS AT DINAMO

When Luka arrived back at Dinamo, there was a great big surprise waiting for him – a ten-year contract!

'We believe that you're the future of this football club,' the club chairman announced. 'We hope you'll be here for a very long time!'

Luka hoped so too. And what was the first thing that he did with his big new contract? That's right – he bought his parents a beautiful home of their own in Zadar.

'This is to say thanks for always believing in me!' Luka told them with tears in his eyes.

The war had been a terrible time for the Modrić

family, but there were good times ahead. Their
golden boy was about to become 'the next Boban'.

It helped that Luka was no longer quite so little.
Those hours hanging from the crossbar had helped;
he was sure of it. He was now 5 feet 8 inches, or
even 5 feet 9 in his football boots.

'I'm taller than Maradona and I'm the same height
as Pelé!' he declared happily.

Luka couldn't wait for the 2005–06 season to
begin. It was going to be a fresh start for Dinamo
after a very disappointing year. There were two main
reasons for the fans to get excited. The club had a
new manager, Josip Kuže, and, most importantly, a
new Number 10, Luka.

'Did you see him play for Zaprešić last season?' the
supporters discussed. 'The guy's a magician!'

There was a lot of pressure on Luka's young
shoulders. Everyone was expecting him to set up
lots of chances for their star strikers, Ivan Bošnjak
and Eduardo. A skilful playmaker – that's what the
team had been missing ever since Niko Kranjčar had
signed for their rivals, Hajduk Split.

Was Luka really the right man for the job? Was he old enough, strong enough, good enough? Of course, but it was time to prove himself yet again.

Dinamo's new attacking trio clicked straight away in training. Luka made the link-up play look so simple.

Control, turn, perfect pass to Ivan… GOAL!

Control, turn, perfect pass to Eduardo… GOAL!

'I've got a good feeling about this!' the Brazilian said with a big smile on his face.

Eduardo had scored ten goals the previous season but with Luka's assists, he hoped to get twice as many.

But could Dinamo's attack play that well in proper matches too? That was the big question and the answer was yes!

In the opening game of the season against HNK Cibalia, Ivan scored the first goal and Vedran scored the second. 2–0 – Dinamo were on fire! Then Luka chested the ball down and calmly smashed it past the goalkeeper.

Goooooooooooooooooooooaaaaaaaaaaaaaaaaalllllllllllllllllllllllllll!!!!!!!!!!!!!!!!!!!!!

Luka felt like he might burst with joy. He had scored his first goal for Dinamo! Another of his football dreams had come true. He celebrated the special moment by doing a cartwheel in front of the chanting fans.

Modrić! Modrić! Modrić!

A new Dinamo star was born.

'What a performance!' Kuže told his team in the dressing room afterwards. 'Now we've got to keep that up.'

Next came: Dinamo 5 Rijeka 0,

And then came: Luka's old team Inter Zaprešić 0 Dinamo 6!

Even after a tough 0–0 draw in the Eternal Derby against Hajduk, Dinamo were still top of the table. And their star Number 10 felt on top of the world.

'We're going all the way,' Luka assured Eduardo. 'This time, the title is ours!'

Away at NK Zagreb, the ball fell to Luka on the edge of the box. He took one touch to control it, then one touch to turn. His third touch was a low left-foot shot, straight into the bottom corner.

Goooooooooooooooooooaaaaaaaaaaaaaaaalllllllllllll lllllllllllllll!!!!!!!!!!!!!!!!!!!!

It was time for Luka to show off his cartwheel celebration again.

Modrić! Modrić! Modrić!

Dinamo were already eleven points clear at the top by the time of the second Eternal Derby of the season. But Luka didn't even think about taking it easy; he wanted revenge for his Hajduk heartbreak.

It was also the battle of Croatia's top two young playmakers – Luka vs Niko Kranjčar. Niko was a year older and already playing for the national team. However, if Luka did well, who knew what might happen? The 2006 World Cup was only a few months away…

The Poljud stadium wasn't a very welcoming place, especially if you played for Dinamo. The Hajduk fans booed every time they touched the ball and their flares filled the air with thick smoke.

'Show no fear!' Kuže had demanded of his team and the Dinamo players listened to their manager.

In the sixtieth minute, Eduardo crossed the ball

into the box and the Hajduk goalkeeper punched it away...

To safety? No!

To Luka? Yes!

Even as three defenders rushed over to close him down, Luka didn't panic. This was his chance for revenge and he wasn't going to waste it. He calmly chested the ball down and then volleyed it into the net.

Gooooooooooooooooooooaaaaaaaaaaaaaaaaalllllllllllll llllllllllllllll!!!!!!!!!!!!!!!!!!!!!

'We're the new KINGS OF CROATIA!' Luka roared as his teammates rushed over to congratulate him. He had never felt an adrenaline rush like it.

Dinamo were crowned champions with two games to spare: Varteks away and then rivals Hajduk at home.

They would be lifting the league title after the final Eternal Derby of the season! That made it even more a must-win game for Dinamo, and the atmosphere at the Maksimir Stadium was incredible. As the supporters clapped their hands and stomped their feet, it was like being inside a loud, beating heart.

Dinamo! Dinamo!

Hajduk! Hajduk!

There was only one goal in the game and guess who scored it? Luka, of course! From the right side of the penalty area, he fired a shot past three defenders, and then the keeper.

Gooooooooooooooooooooaaaaaaaaaaaaaaaaalllllllllllll lllllllllllll!!!!!!!!!!!!!!!!!!!!

What a way to end his first Dinamo season! As the stadium erupted, Luka jumped over the advertising boards to celebrate with the fans. He threw his shirt high into the air and jogged around the running track on a lap of honour, with his teammates trailing behind.

In his very first season as Dinamo's Number 10, Luka had become a Croatian League winner and a true club hero. Thirty-three games, seven goals, and lots of awesome assists. What he needed now was a relaxing holiday but he had to cancel his summer plans.

Instead, Luka was off to Germany!

CHAPTER 11

CROATIA

With Luka playing so well for his club, it was only a matter of time before he started playing for his country.

Croatia had talented defenders and strikers but they were missing a touch of magic in midfield. It had been that way ever since Boban's retirement after the 1998 World Cup.

'Modrić is our best playmaker by miles!' the Dinamo fans said of their Number 10.

'Yeah, he's way better than Niko Kranjčar. If he wasn't the manager's son, he wouldn't even be in the squad!'

It was true that Croatia's coach, Zlatko Kranjčar,

was Niko's dad, but he didn't let that affect his decisions. He was simply looking for the best footballers in the country to take to the 2006 World Cup. There was no doubt that Luka was now on that list. So in March 2006, Kranjčar called him up for their friendly match against Argentina.

When his phone rang, Luka knew who it would be. With trembling hands, he answered and listened.

'Wow, thank you, it's such an honour!' he told the Croatia coach. 'I can't wait to play for my country.'

That had been Luka's dream ever since watching Bilić, Boban and Šuker at Euro 96. As soon as the call ended, he shared the news with his parents.

'Congratulations!' they screamed. 'We're so proud of you, son.'

The timing was perfect. Luka knew that if he did a good job against Lionel Messi and co., he had a great chance of making Croatia's World Cup squad. Even if he didn't get to play at the tournament in Germany, it would still be the trip of a lifetime.

'I can do this!' Luka told himself as he set off to join the squad.

Sadly, he wouldn't be making his Croatia debut in front of a loud home crowd, but never mind. All Luka really cared about was playing football for his country. He had worked hard for this moment and he felt ready to shine. Zrinjski, Zaprešić, Dinamo – he had a lot more experience than most twenty-year-olds!

When Kranjčar announced his starting XI to face Argentina, Luka's name was there alongside Niko's in midfield.

'I want to see if you two can play together in the same team,' the manager told them. Luka would be in central midfield, with Niko further forward in the Number 10 role.

'No problem,' Luka thought. He would have played anywhere for his country, even in goal!

It turned out to be a very exciting game indeed. Croatia scored first but Messi soon turned things around. At half-time, it was 2–1 to Argentina. Luka was disappointed with himself as he entered the dressing room. Where was his usual Dinamo magic? He needed to find it fast.

'Come on, this isn't over yet,' Kranjčar told his

team. 'Keep attacking!'

As the game went on, Luka got more and more involved in the action. He didn't manage to get a goal or an assist but he played a key part in the Croatia comeback.

2–2, then 3–2 to the Chequered Ones!

What a victory for Croatia! At the final whistle, the players formed a long line across the pitch and ran over to their fans.

'Hurray!' they cheered together, throwing their arms up in the air.

So, was Luka now part of the Croatia team? Was he on his way to the World Cup? Yes! After playing in three more friendlies, Luka made it into Kranjčar's squad.

'Yes! We're off to Germany!' he screamed with his Dinamo teammate, Ivan.

What a year it had already been for Luka, and he still had the greatest football tournament to go. He had high hopes for his World Cup adventure. Could Croatia do even better than their heroes of 1998, and get to the final?

No matter what, Luka was determined to make the most of every minute. After all, World Cups didn't come around every day!

Croatia's opening match would be against the 2002 champions Brazil. That meant taking on Kaká, Ronaldinho, Adriano *and* Ronaldo. Luka thought back to his first pair of shin pads, which had pictures of Brazil's star striker on them. The little kid from Zadar had come a very long way since then!

For that first game, the Croatia coach was more focused on defending than attacking. So, Luka had to watch and wait on the bench.

Captain Niko Kovač came off injured... but Kranjčar brought on Jerko Leko instead.

'That's fair enough,' Luka thought, 'we need a tough-tackling midfielder against these guys.'

But then Croatia went 1-0 down... and Kranjčar brought on Ivica Olić instead.

The minutes ticked by, but Croatia couldn't find an equaliser.

'Bring me on! Bring me on!' Luka muttered under his breath.

They still had one substitution left, but their manager chose not to use it.

'Never mind,' Luka told himself, trying to stay positive. 'We've still got at least two more games to go.'

Luka played the last fifteen minutes against Japan, and then the last twenty against Australia. He did his very best to recreate his Dinamo magic but sadly, he just couldn't be the super sub that his nation needed. After two disappointing draws and one defeat, Croatia were heading home early.

'No, I'm so much better than that!' Luka scolded himself. He had now played in seven matches for Croatia without scoring a single goal, or setting one up for the strikers.

As the team trudged off the pitch in Stuttgart, the captain Niko noticed that their youngest player was distraught.

'Hey, you'll be back to fight again in four years,' he reassured Luka. Niko was thirty-four, so it was probably the end of his own World Cup dream. 'And before that, we've got Euro 2008 to win!'

CHAPTER 12

LUKA & EDUARDO

Before the start of the new season, Dinamo sold
Ivan to Belgian team Genk. Their amazing attacking
trio had now become a duo, but a very deadly duo
indeed – Luka and Eduardo.

The other football clubs in Croatia didn't stand a
chance. In the Super Cup final, Dinamo destroyed
Rijeka.

Luka fired a shot into the bottom right corner. 2–0!

Eduardo scored from the penalty spot. 3–1!

Luka passed to Davor Vugrinec, who passed to
Eduardo. 4–1!

'What a way to start the new season!' Luka
cheered.

'That's just trophy number one,' Eduardo added.
'We've still got three more to go!'

Dinamo were aiming to win everything: the
Croatian League title again, plus the Croatian
Cup and even the Champions League. Lifting the
Champions League trophy would be a really, really
tough challenge, but with Luka and Eduardo in
attack, anything seemed possible.

'Come on, we can do it!' urged their new manager
Branko Ivanković.

Dinamo's first opponents were English giants,
Arsenal. Luka would be up against another excellent
young playmaker – Cesc Fàbregas. Who would come
out on top?

In the first leg in Zagreb, Luka created lots of
chances for Dinamo, but Fàbregas won the battle
of the midfield maestros. He scored two goals as
Arsenal won 3–0.

'Never mind, we've now got nothing to lose in
London!' Ivanković told his players.

Eduardo scored an early goal at Arsenal's new
Emirates Stadium, but that was the end of Dinamo's

Champions League dream. It was a learning experience for all of them, but especially for Luka. He was desperate to raise his game to that next level.

'Hey, when we win the league, we'll get another chance next year!' he reminded his disappointed teammates.

Dinamo stormed through the Croatian league season, winning their first eight games in a row. Eduardo scored most of the goals, and Luka got most of the assists. What a perfect partnership!

'Do you even need the rest of us?' Vedran joked.

Soon, there were only two teams in the title race – Dinamo and Hajduk. Their old rivals were still only three points behind. One defeat and they'd be tied at the top.

'Come on, we can't let that happen!' Ivanković told his players.

Luka loved pinging perfect passes to Eduardo, but when his team needed him, he could be a goalscorer too.

Against NK Zagreb, Dinamo were winning 1–0 with ten minutes to go. But would one goal be enough? Although their defence was strong, they were up against Croatia's new star striker, Mario Mandžukić. A second goal would really make things safe, and keep them ahead of Hajduk...

As Dinamo attacked down the left wing, Luka took up his favourite position, right on the edge of the box. He was so smart that he knew exactly where the ball would end up. As it rolled towards him, the fans cried out, 'Shooooooot!'

'Don't worry!' Luka thought to himself. He knew what he needed to do, but he wasn't going to rush it.

Left foot control, right side-foot shot,

Goooooooooooooooooooaaaaaaaaaaaaaaaaallllllllllll llllllllllllll!!!!!!!!!!!!!!!!!!!

'Nice one, Luka!' Eduardo cheered as his friend jumped up into his arms.

Modrić! Modrić! Modrić!

Luka was the fans' favourite player. He wasn't just a hero; he was a *super*hero because he always saved the day. That goal turned out to be very important because Mandžukić scored for NK Zagreb a few minutes later.

At the final whistle, Luka walked around the Maksimir Stadium, clapping the supporters. They understood now; the biggest guys weren't always the best players.

Modrić! Modrić! Modrić!

It still gave him a real thrill to hear them chanting his name, and to see little kids wearing Dinamo shirts with '10 MODRIC' on the back.

'I was one of those kids not so long ago!' he liked to remind himself.

Luka was soon saving the day again. In the semi-finals of the Croatian Cup, Dinamo were losing 2–1 to Hajduk with twenty minutes to go. Was their cup dream over? Not with Luka on the pitch!

He chased onto Sammir's pass and slid the ball beautifully past the goalkeeper.

Goooooooooooooaaaaaaaaaalllllllllllllllllllllll!!!!!!!!!!!!!

2–2 – thanks to Luka, they were back in the game! Then in the ninetieth minute, Josip Tadić scored Dinamo's winning goal.

'I knew we could do it!' Luka celebrated, punching the air passionately.

75

The Treble was still on for Dinamo. They had already won the Super Cup, they were into the Croatian Cup final, and the league title was getting closer and closer.

Dinamo 1 Osijek 0,

Pula 1 Dinamo 2,

Dinamo 4 Cibalia 0...

With one more win away at bottom club Kamen Ingrad, they would be crowned the Champions of Croatia again. But after an hour of attacking, Dinamo still hadn't scored. The fans were getting restless.

'Come on, why aren't we beating this lot?' they shouted.

'Right, I'll sort this,' Luka decided. At the age of twenty-one, he was already a team leader.

Left foot control, right foot dipping half-volley,

Gooooooooooooooooooooaaaaaaaaaaaaaaaaallllllllllllll llllllllllllll!!!!!!!!!!!!!!!!!!!

That was it; the league title was theirs!

'You beauty!' Luka's teammates cried out, lifting him high into the air.

A few weeks later, Dinamo completed the Treble

by beating Slaven Belupo 2–1 in the cup final.

What a season it had been! As the team posed for photos with their trophies, there were two smiling faces right at the front: Luka and Eduardo, the league's Player of the Year and the league's top goalscorer.

Could Dinamo hold on to their deadly duo? Sadly not. Eduardo got a big move to Arsenal, but Luka decided to stay put, at least for one more season.

He would miss his friend but he had a new strike partner now – Mario Mandžukić. They weren't quite as deadly as Luka and Eduardo, but Dinamo still won the Croatian League and Cup double again. Luka was the boy with the golden touch, after all.

CHAPTER 13

EURO 08

Just days after the disappointment of the 2006 World Cup, Luka received some very good news. The new national team manager would be Slaven Bilić, one of Croatia's greatest ever defenders and Luka's old coach with the Under-21s.

Tomislav Bašić and Slaven Bilić – they were the two managers who had believed in him most. From day one, Bilić had been blown away by Luka the little magician.

'You can be one of the best midfielders in the world,' Bilić told him, back when he was only nineteen.

Two years later, the new Croatia manager's

message hadn't changed. 'You're going to be my main man. In my opinion, you're up there with Xavi and Andrés Iniesta!'

That praise gave Luka lots of confidence. In Bilić's first game in charge, Luka scored his first international goal in a 2–0 win over Italy. When the goalkeeper spilled a long-range shot, he was the first to react. His shot crashed off the crossbar and bounced down over the line.

Goooooooooooooooooooaaaaaaaaaaaaaaaalllllllllllll llllllllllllllll!!!!!!!!!!!!!!!!!!!!

'Nice one, Luka!' Eduardo cheered.

They weren't playing for the same club anymore, but the deadly duo were reunited for their country. And their next target? Qualification for Euro 2008!

To make it to the tournament, Croatia would need to finish top of Group E, above Russia, Israel *and* England. The Three Lions had a team full of world superstars: John Terry, Rio Ferdinand, Frank Lampard, David Beckham, Steven Gerrard, Wayne Rooney… It wouldn't be easy but if Bilić believed, then so did Luka!

In front of a roaring home crowd in Zagreb, he dribbled down the left wing and curled a high cross towards his strike partner. Eduardo had two defenders around him, but he managed to head it up over the keeper and into the net. 1–0 to Croatia!

'You're the best, Luka!' Eduardo shouted as they celebrated yet another goal together.

Bilić's boys were unstoppable. They even won in the pouring rain at Wembley, beating England 3–2. At the final whistle, the Croatian players threw their arms up triumphantly.

'Euro 2008, here we come!' they cheered.

Luka couldn't wait. This time, he would be going to a major tournament as Croatia's first-choice playmaker. His country would be counting on him to produce as much magic as possible, especially without Eduardo, who had suffered a horrible injury at Arsenal.

'Don't worry, we're going to bring that trophy home for you!' Luka promised his heartbroken friend.

The players were fully focused on making their nation proud. There were red and white chequers everywhere! Thousands of Croatians had travelled to

Austria to support their team.

And they soon had something to cheer about. In the third minute, Luka battled bravely against a big Austria defender near the corner flag. Somehow, he managed to escape with the ball and pass to Ivica Olić, who raced into the box and… *FOUL – penalty to Croatia!*

But who would take it? Bilić had given the big responsibility to his main man – Luka!

'I can do this!' he told himself as he waited for the referee's whistle. All he had to was stay calm and pick his spot…

Goooooooooooooooooooaaaaaaaaaaaaaaaaallllllllllll llllllllllllllll!!!!!!!!!!!!!!!!!!!

As the goalkeeper dived left, Luka placed his shot straight down the middle. What a cool penalty, and what a start to Euro 2008! He ran towards the fans, pumping his fists like crazy.

Croatia! Croatia! Croatia!

Luka's penalty turned out to be the only goal of the game. Croatia were off the mark with a win but Bilić wasn't satisfied with his team's performance.

'That was good but not good enough,' the manager told his players afterwards. 'Come on, we can play so much better than that!'

They would need to be at their best to beat their next opponents – Germany. It was 1–1 in their big tournament battle. Germany had won the Euro 96 quarter-final, but Croatia had got sweet revenge at the 1998 World Cup. Ten years later, who would be victorious this time?

Germany had Michael Ballack and Torsten Frings in the middle, but they were no match for Luka. Not when he was playing one of the best games of his life. He was absolutely amazing!

When he didn't have the ball, Luka was like a busy bee, buzzing around the pitch to win it back.

Then, when he did have the ball, Luka turned into a calm midfield maestro. He skipped past every tackle, pinging passes left and right, long and short. He was the classiest player on the pitch and he didn't give the ball away, not even once!

With their star playmaker controlling everything, Croatia pushed forward on the attack...

Danijel Pranjić swung the ball into the six-yard box and Darijo Srna poked it in. 1–0!

Ivan Rakitić's cross deflected off a defender, then off the post, and fell right at Ivica's feet. 2–0!

The Croatian fans were in dreamland. They danced in their seats at the Wörthersee Stadium, and in the streets back home.

It wasn't over yet, though. Luka kept going until the very end. He passed, he dribbled, he tackled, he intercepted. He was the man of the match by miles.

Germany did pull one goal back, but not two. At the final whistle, the Croatian players hugged like never before. Then they formed a long line across the pitch and ran over to their fans.

'We did it!' they cried, throwing their arms up in the air. 'We're into the quarter-finals!'

It was one of the best nights of Luka's life. He was living out his dream, following in the footsteps of Croatian national heroes at Euro 96 and World Cup 98.

'Two more wins and we're in the final!' Bilić reminded them.

But first things first – they had to get past Turkey.

As the Croatian anthem rang out in the Ernst Happel Stadium, Luka sang along with his hand on his heart. Representing his country meant so much to him. Could he help make his people proud?

Luka carried on his brilliant form from the Germany game. He dribbled into the penalty area and crossed to Ivica. His shot cannoned back off the crossbar and then Niko could only head the rebound wide.

'Nooooo!' Luka groaned, pounding the ground in frustration. What a golden chance wasted!

He created lots more chances but after ninety minutes, the score was still 0–0.

'Keep going!' his manager urged him. 'The goal will come!'

Right at the end of extra-time, Luka thought he had won it for Croatia. The ball seemed to be rolling out for a corner but he managed to keep it in and chip a lovely left-foot cross to Ivan Klasnić. 1–0!

Their wild celebrations didn't last long, however. Turkey went down the other end and equalised. 1–1 – the game was going to penalties!

Luka couldn't believe it but he had to get over the shock quickly. It was his job to take Croatia's first spot kick.

'I scored against Austria and I'm going to score again here,' Luka told himself as he made the long walk forward.

This time, he aimed for the bottom right corner, but his shot flew wide of the post.

Luka felt sick to his stomach as he walked away with his head in his hands. What a terrible mistake!

'Don't worry,' his teammates tried to comfort him, 'we can still win this.'

But they couldn't. The Turkey keeper saved Mladen Petrić's penalty to win the shoot-out.

The Croatian players just sat there, speechless and sprawled out on the grass. They were out, their dream was over, and the pain was incredible.

It took a long time but eventually, Luka looked back happily on his big international breakthrough. His excellent performances had earned him a place in the Team of the Tournament. Just like Eduardo predicted, Luka had really made a name for himself at Euro 2008.

CHAPTER 14

LONDON CALLING

The Tottenham Hotspur chairman Daniel Levy watched Euro 2008 with a big grin on his face. That little Croatian magician who was making Germany look like fools? He was a Spurs player now!

Yes, before the 2007–08 club season ended, Luka had made up his mind. He was signing for Tottenham.

The English club had been watching Luka for ages. Their European scout, Riccardo Pecini, had first spotted him during his early days at Dinamo.

'He's not the biggest, but boy can the kid play!' Pecini told Damien Comolli, Tottenham's Director of Football. 'I think he'd be the perfect playmaker for us.'

As soon as Comolli saw Luka in action, he fell
in love. The terrific touch, the clever passes, the
silky skills, the exciting energy – what a fantastic
footballer! It was easy to imagine Luka running the
show for Tottenham. He had the talent to become
one of the best midfielders in the Premier League.

'The fans are going to love Luka!' he thought to
himself.

Comolli started talking to Dinamo straight away,
but Tottenham waited for the right time to make their
move. There was no hurry – or was there? One day,
Levy got a worried call from the Director of Football.

'Daniel, if we don't act fast, we're going to lose
Modrić to Manchester City,' Comolli explained.
There was also talk of interest from Arsenal, Chelsea
and Barcelona. 'We can't let that happen!'

'No problem, leave it with me,' the Tottenham
chairman replied calmly.

Levy flew straight to Zagreb in his private jet. He
was ready to do business and bring Luka to White
Hart Lane. After a long day of discussions, he made a
late phone call to Comolli.

'Damien, we've got our man!'

Luka had considered lots of other offers too, but this one felt like the right one for him. Tottenham were a big Premier League club with big ambitions for the future. Their manager Juande Ramos wanted them to challenge for all the top trophies, in England and in Europe.

'But to do that, we're going to need more quality players like you!' Ramos explained.

Luka knew that it was time for him to move on and test himself at a higher level. He was nearly twenty-three now, and what was there left for him to achieve in Croatia? During his three years in the Dinamo first team, Luka had won everything: three league titles, two Croatian Cups, one Croatian Super Cup, and one Croatian League Player of the Year award.

'Thank you!' Luka shouted as he waved goodbye at the Maksimir Stadium.

'Thank *you*!' the Dinamo fans shouted back. They stood and clapped their hero off the pitch. 'We'll always love you, Luka!'

Now, London was calling, and it helped that Luka already had a good friend living there.

'Welcome, we'll be neighbours again now!' Eduardo cheered. After his awful injury, he was trying to fight his way back into the Arsenal team.

When Luka arrived in England, he knew that expectations would be high. Tottenham had paid £16million for him, which was a new club record fee. However, after his performances at Euro 2008, he looked worth every penny.

'What a bargain!' Levy chuckled to himself. Thank goodness for that quick trip to Zagreb. 'Real Madrid and Barcelona would probably pay £30million for him now!'

Luka was Tottenham's top summer signing but he wasn't the only one. The club also bought Brazilian goalkeeper Heurelho Gomes from PSV Eindhoven and Mexican forward Giovani dos Santos from Barcelona.

'These are the quality players that we need to challenge for the Premier League title!' Ramos declared.

That quality had to be tested first, though. At training, Tottenham's tough-tackling midfielder Jamie O'Hara took one look at Luka and thought, 'Yes, he's skilful, but he's so small! I'll be able to push him off the ball easily.'

But he thought wrong. Luka was a lot stronger than he looked, both physically and mentally. The war in Croatia, the Hajduk heartbreak, the season in Bosnia – all those experiences had toughened him up.

O'Hara ran and ran but he just couldn't get the ball. With his terrific first touch, Luka was able to escape every time.

'It's like he's always thinking three steps ahead!' O'Hara groaned with a mix of frustration and respect.

'He's a little magician,' Jermaine Jenas agreed. 'I'm just glad that he'll be playing *for* us, rather than *against* us!'

Off the training pitch, Luka tried his best to settle in quickly. He explored London with Eduardo and Vedran, who had just joined him at Tottenham.

He also worked hard to improve his English, and
especially his football vocabulary:

Man-on!

Down the line!

Foul, ref!

Luka still missed his family and friends back in
Croatia, but this was his home now and he had a
job to do. He was going to become a Premier League
superstar. He couldn't wait to make his Tottenham
debut in the first match of the 2008–09 season, away
at Middlesbrough.

'Are you ready for this?' Jermaine asked as they
took up their positions for kick-off. They would be
playing together in central midfield.

'Of course!' Luka replied.

He was buzzing with adrenaline but nothing
could have prepared him for the pace of the Premier
League. Wow, they were playing football at 100
miles per hour! He could hear the rushing noise in
his ears:

'*Whoooooooosh!*'

It was fast and furious, but Luka showed no fear.

He just needed to do what he had always done – at Zadar, at Zrinjski, at Zaprešić, and at Dinamo. With quick thinking and a terrific first touch, he could escape every time...

CRUNCH! A Middlesbrough midfielder slid in for the tackle and sent Luka flying.

'Welcome to England!' his teammate David Bentley joked, helping him back up to his feet.

Luka tried his best to stay cool and composed but every time he got the ball, he was surrounded by big guys snapping at his heels. Help! What was he meant to do?

'Play your passes quickly!' Jermaine shouted.

Luka wasn't playing in the Croatian League anymore. If he wanted to become a Premier League superstar, he would need to change his game. As a youngster, he had taught himself to think fast to avoid the fouls; now, he needed to teach himself to think even faster.

CHAPTER 15

TURNING IT AROUND AT TOTTENHAM

Luka got better as the game against Middlesbrough went on, but Tottenham still lost 2–1. It was a bad start to the season and things soon got even worse.

Tottenham 1 Sunderland 2,

Tottenham 1 Aston Villa 2,

Portsmouth 2 Tottenham 0...

After eight games, Tottenham were bottom of the league with only two points. Uh oh, they were in big, big trouble.

'I can't believe that we still haven't won a single game,' Vedran complained. 'Why are we playing so badly?'

Luka wished that he had the answer to that

question. He was meant to be Tottenham's midfield maestro but so far, he had zero goals and one assist.

'That's nowhere *near* good enough!' Luka admitted.

The English newspapers were saying the same old things about him:

'Modrić is too lightweight for the Premier League.'

'Modrić looks like a lost little boy in the Tottenham midfield.'

But Luka stayed strong. After all, he had heard it all before back in Croatia. He knew that none of it was true; he was just getting used to a different style of football. It inspired him to work even harder to prove people wrong.

It didn't help that Ramos was asking him to play a different position every week. Central midfield, then left wing, then Number 10, then central midfield again...

Everything improved, however, once Harry Redknapp arrived. On his first day, the new Tottenham manager watched his players closely during training. The club was in a relegation fight

now, and so Redknapp was looking for players with
spirit, as well as skill.

There was one player who stood out from the
crowd. With his quick thinking and terrific first
touch, Luka was running the show.

Touch, turn, perfect pass,

Touch, turn, perfect pass.

It was a joy to watch Luka pass and move. He
never stopped running and calling for the ball. Then,
when he spotted some space ahead of him:

Control, turn, dribble, SHOOT,

Goooooooooooooooooooooaaaaaaaaaaaaaaaalllllllllllll
lllllllllllllll!!!!!!!!!!!!!!!!!!!!!!

Redknapp breathed a big sigh of relief. 'With
Modrić in midfield, there's no way we're going
down!' he thought to himself.

The Tottenham turnaround began straight away
against Bolton. Luka pushed forward, linking up
brilliantly with the team's striker, Darren Bent. When
Luka's shot was saved, Darren ran in for the rebound
but the keeper brought him down... Penalty – 2–0
to Tottenham!

'That's more like it!' Luka cried out with passion.

That victory gave them some confidence going into their next game – the big North London Derby. It was the match that Luka had been looking forward to. He had heard so much about the rivalry and the amazing atmosphere.

Tottenham scored an early goal but with only five minutes to go, Arsenal were winning 4–2.

'Come on, keep going!' Jermaine clapped and cheered. 'It's not over yet!'

He won the ball in midfield and dribbled forward. 'Shoooot!' the fans urged and on the edge of the penalty area, Jermaine did just that. *GOAL – 4–3!*

'What did I tell you?' he said with a smile. 'See, it's not over yet!'

No it wasn't, and Luka was determined to make his mark. In the last minute, he chested the ball down, turned and fired a brilliant shot at goal. Luka watched with excitement as it swerved through the air, towards the top corner...

But no, it struck the post instead! So close,

but luckily Aaron Lennon was there to score the rebound. *4–4!*

It was party time for Tottenham! Aaron ran and dived across the grass, with Luka right behind.

'What a cool finish!'

'Hey man, it was your shot that created the chance. You're a hero too!'

Things were finally looking up for Luka and Tottenham. They beat Liverpool and Manchester City to move out of the relegation zone.

Hurray! That was great but Luka was still searching for his first Premier League goal. Game 10, Game 11, Game 12... the wait went on and on. He was taking lots of shots but the ball just wouldn't go in.

'This is getting ridiculous!' he moaned to Vedran. 'I scored seventeen goals for Dinamo last season.'

'If it makes you feel any better, I haven't scored either.'

'Yeah, but you're a right-back!'

Four days before Christmas, Luka's big moment finally arrived. What a perfect present! In the thirtieth minute, defender Michael Dawson played a great ball over the top of the Newcastle United defence. Luka was off, chasing after it at top speed!

On the edge of the box, he slowed down a little. Sébastien Bassong was catching up with him, but Luka refused to rush and waste such a glorious chance.

Right foot control, right foot shot past the keeper! Gooooooooooooooooooooaaaaaaaaaaaaaaaaaallllllllllll lllllllllllllll!!!!!!!!!!!!!!!!!!!!

Luka ran over to the corner flag and jumped for joy. 'At last!' he cried out at the top of his lungs.

It was a real relief to score for Tottenham, but Luka still didn't feel like he was back to his Dinamo and Euro 2008 best. Not yet. Every week, he worked harder and harder. And every week, he got closer and closer…

…Until Chelsea came to White Hart Lane in March 2009. Luka knew from his very first kick that it was going to be a good day. No, a *great* day.

He felt calm, confident and full of energy. In no time, he was controlling the game. Whenever Luka got the ball, it was like he had all the time in the world.

Control, turn, perfect pass,

Control, turn, dribble,

Control, turn, dribble then perfect pass!

The Tottenham fans were loving it. They cheered every time he touched the ball.

Modrić! Modrić! Modrić!

Early in the second half, Aaron raced down the right wing and crossed it into Luka's favourite area – just inside the penalty area. He didn't even take a touch to control it; that's how confident he was feeling. He just struck the ball first time into the bottom corner.

Goooooooooooooooooooaaaaaaaaaaaaaaaalllllllllllll llllllllllllllll!!!!!!!!!!!!!!!!!!!!

'Yes, yes, YES!' Luka ran past his delighted teammates and dived across the White Hart Lane grass. Finally, he had found his best form in England.

CHAPTER 16

PREMIER LEAGUE PLAYMAKER

By the end of his first season in England, Luka had five goals and ten assists. He wasn't delighted, but he was satisfied. They were pretty good numbers for a new Premier League playmaker. Tottenham had finished in eighth place, a whopping twenty-one points away from their Top Four target.

'Hey, that's not bad considering we were bottom after eight games!' Vedran argued. 'And we only lost the League Cup final on penalties.'

'You're right,' Luka agreed. 'Next season, we've got to win at least one trophy for sure!'

There was now a third Croatian at Tottenham too. Redknapp had signed Luka's old national team rival,

Niko, from Portsmouth, to add another attacking option.

'Not you again!' the two playmakers joked together. 'Hopefully, Mr Redknapp will let us play in the same team this time.'

One thing was certain; Luka wasn't giving up his Spurs starting spot without a fight. On the opening day of the 2009–10 season, against Liverpool, Tottenham's midfield looked brilliantly balanced. Wilson Palacios had the power, Tom Huddlestone had the passing, Aaron Lennon had the pace, and Luka? He had the magic touch!

He created chance after chance for his teammates, but the strikers had left their shooting boots at home. In the second half, Luka curled a teasing free kick into the penalty area and Sébastien Bassong headed it home. Yes, they were off to a winning start!

'What a ball, mate!' Aaron said to Luka as the players celebrated together in front of the fans.

Three more wins later, and Tottenham were top of the table! Luka, however, was on the treatment table, and the news wasn't good.

'I'm afraid you've fractured your right leg,' the club physio told him after doing a series of tests.

Nooooooo! Luka's heart sank. The timing was terrible, just when he was playing his best football for Tottenham. He had never really had a serious injury before. 'How long will I be out for?' he asked with his fingers firmly crossed.

He was hoping that the answer would be a few weeks, but no. 'A few months,' the physio predicted.

September, October and November were long, lonely months for Luka. Tottenham missed their midfield playmaker, but he missed them even more.

'I never really realised how much I love playing football until now,' Luka admitted to Vedran and Niko. They did their best to cheer him up as he worked his way back to fitness. Luka had always hated the gym but that's where he spent his days, building up the strength in his leg again.

'You're nearly there now!' the physio said to keep him motivated.

Finally, Luka was ready to return. He couldn't wait to feel the football buzz again. 'Let's go out there and win!' he shouted in the dressing room before kick-off.

Aaron raced down the right wing and crossed it into Luka's favourite area – just inside the penalty area. He was unmarked, with the goal in front of him…

Luka volleyed the ball over the diving West Ham keeper, using the right leg that he had broken.

Goooooooooooooooooooooaaaaaaaaaaaaaaaaaallllllllllll lllllllllllllll!!!!!!!!!!!!!!!!!!!!!

Luka rushed straight over to the Tottenham fans with a huge smile on his face. His comeback was complete.

'It's great to have you back!' Aaron hugged him.

'It's great to *be* back!' Luka replied.

2010 was going to be his big breakthrough. It was going to be the year when he became a top Premier League playmaker.

Luka crossed to Peter Crouch… *GOAL!*

Luka dribbled forward until he ran out of room. No problem, he looked up and picked out Roman Pavlyuchenko with a perfect pass… *GOAL!*

Luka slipped another clever ball through to Roman... *GOAL!*

Luka collected Crouchy's flick and fed it to Eiður Guðjohnsen... *GOAL!*

'It's so much fun playing with you,' Tottenham's strikers all told him. 'We wouldn't swap you for anyone; not even Iniesta or Fàbregas!'

'Luka is a truly world-class talent,' Redknapp declared proudly, 'and he's as brave as a lion.'

Finally, people in England had stopped talking about Luka's size and strength. And finally, they had stopped asking whether he could handle life in the Premier League. Of course he could!

With his confidence sky high, Luka carried on creating all kinds of magic.

Against Everton, Niko passed to him on the edge of the area. Three defenders tried to close him down but he skipped through and chipped the keeper.

Goooooooooooooooooooooaaaaaaaaaaaaaaaalllllllllllll llllllllllllll!!!!!!!!!!!!!!!!!!!

Against Burnley, he danced his way into the box. Stepover to the right, then a shift to the left and...

Gooooooooooooooooooooaaaaaaaaaaaaaaaallllllllllll llllllllllllll!!!!!!!!!!!!!!!!!!

Daniel Levy, the Tottenham chairman, was delighted to see Luka in such fantastic form. There was just one problem; the top clubs in Europe were paying attention too.

Manchester United, for example, needed a new playmaker to replace Paul Scholes.

'Modrić would be perfect!' their fans thought and Sir Alex Ferguson seemed to agree.

No way! Once again, Levy had to act fast. He met with Luka and agreed a big new six-year contract. Hurray, their star playmaker was staying!

'I have no interest in going anywhere,' Luka told the media. 'Tottenham gave me my chance in the Premier League and I want to go on to achieve great success here.'

There was no way that he could leave before the club's most exciting season for years. After finishing fourth, Tottenham were into the Champions League!

CHAPTER 17

CHAMPIONS LEAGUE

Luka had played in the Champions League qualifying rounds during his Dinamo days, but they had never made it through to the group stage. Could he finally reach the real competition this time with Tottenham?

'Come on, we *have* to get there!' Luka told Aaron. It was his dream to play in Europe's top tournament, and he couldn't bear to miss out yet again.

BSC Young Boys in Switzerland were the last team standing in their way. Tottenham lost the first leg, away, but they won at White Hart Lane, thanks to a hat-trick from Crouchy. They had done it; they were into the Champions League Group Stage for the first time ever.

'Nice one, mate!' Luka cheered, stretching up to hug his extremely tall teammate. Their little and large partnership was going to be key to Tottenham's success.

Luka was always looking to take his game to the next level. That's why he had left Zadar to join Dinamo, and why he had moved from Croatia to play in the English Premier League.

Now, that next level was the Champions League. Luka loved everything about the competition: the logo, the anthem, the history, and especially the top-quality teams. In Group A, Tottenham would be taking on German giants Werder Bremen, Dutch champions FC Twente, and Italian champions Inter Milan.

'This is it, lads,' Redknapp told his players before their first game. 'Football games don't get much bigger than this!'

Luka was out injured for the 2–2 draw away at Werder Bremen, but he was back in the team to take on Twente. He couldn't wait. As he walked into the dressing room at White Hart Lane, there was his white shirt hanging in the corner, with '14 MODRIC' on the back. And on the right sleeve, there was the Champions League logo. The sight of it sent excited shivers down Luka's spine.

Once the game kicked off, however, he was the same calm playmaker as always.

Control, turn, perfect pass,

Control, turn, perfect pass.

Luka was a Champions League natural! It helped that Tottenham now had more attacking options than ever. When he got the ball in central midfield, Luka had Gareth Bale flying down the left wing, Rafael van der Vaart ahead in the Number 10 role, and Crouchy up top. It was goal time almost every time!

After a 4–1 win against Twente, the Tottenham players felt confident about their trip to Milan. Why not?

'We've got nothing to fear!' their manager told them.

Eight minutes into the game, however, Tottenham

had plenty to fear. They were 1–0 down, their goalkeeper had been sent off, and Inter had a penalty. Uh oh, they were in big, big trouble.

Redknapp needed to bring on his sub keeper, Carlo Cudicini, but who would he bring off? Crouchy? Jermaine? No, he took off Luka, his little midfield magician.

'I'm sorry to do this to you,' his manager said as he trudged slowly off the San Siro pitch.

Luka understood but he couldn't help feeling disappointed, especially when Gareth sparked an incredible second-half comeback.

4–1, 4–2, 4–3!

If Luka had still been out there, pulling the strings, it could have been even better.

'If only!' he thought to himself.

Two weeks later, it was time for the rematch in London. Luka rubbed his hands with glee. This time, he was going to play every single minute, and he was going to put on a midfield masterclass.

Luka dribbled at the Inter defence. Stepover to the right, shift to the left, left-foot shot and… *SAVED!*

'Unlucky, keep going!' Crouchy encouraged him.

Luka soon danced his way through again and this time, he spotted Rafael's run. Of course, the pass was perfect – 1–0 to Tottenham!

Rafael raced over to celebrate with the fans but he saved a special hug for Luka. 'That ball was unreal!' he cried out.

Now that Tottenham had the lead, Luka sat deeper in midfield and let the speedy wingers do the running. Gareth on the left and Aaron on the right; they were far too fast for Inter.

Gareth crossed to Crouchy – 2–0!

Gareth crossed to Roman – 3–1!

At the final whistle, Luka threw his arms up into the air and celebrated with his teammates. What a win! The Tottenham players and fans were in dreamland. If they could beat Werder Bremen, they would be through to the Champions League Round of 16...

In the last minute of the first half, Crouchy headed the ball down to Luka on the edge of the box. As the Bremen defender jumped to block the shot, Luka

coolly shifted it from left foot to right foot,
then BANG!

*Goooooooooooooooooooooaaaaaaaaaaaaaaaaalllllllllllll
llllllllllllllllll!!!!!!!!!!!!!!!!!!!!!*

Luka punched the air and then jumped into
Crouchy's arms. He had his first Champions League
goal, and his team had the victory they needed.

'Come on, you Spurs!' the fans chanted all night
long.

In the Round of 16, Tottenham would be heading
back to Italy, this time to play AC Milan. Their team
was packed with superstars: Alessandro Nesta,
Clarence Seedorf, Robinho, Zlatan Ibrahimović…
The list of big names went on and on.

'Yeah, but we've got top players too!' the
Tottenham supporters argued.

Gareth was their new standout star, but Luka was
a close second. With his quick thinking and terrific
first touch, he could change any game.

Luka wasn't fit enough to start the away leg at the
San Siro, but he was desperate to play his part. So,
with thirty minutes to go, Redknapp brought him

on. Tottenham were defending bravely but if they could just score an away goal, it would be the perfect result...

On the counter-attack, Sandro passed to Luka, who passed it through two Milan midfielders to set Aaron free. *ZOOM!* He was off, flying up the wing. Aaron skipped past one tackle and then crossed to Crouchy. *GOAL!*

Suddenly, the Tottenham corner of the stadium exploded into life. They were winning away in Italy! Crouchy blew kisses to the crowd and then ran over to thank the creators: Aaron and Luka.

'Lads, we did it!' he screamed.

That turned out to be the winning goal. After a tense 0–0 draw at White Hart Lane, Tottenham were through to the Champions League quarter-finals!

Unfortunately, their next opponents were Real Madrid. They were no match for the Galácticos, especially once Crouchy had been sent off.

That was the end of Tottenham's amazing 2010–11 European adventure, but they left with heads held high. They could be very proud of their efforts and achievements.

Luka was sure that he would be back soon. After his first taste of the Champions League, he was greedy for more.

CHAPTER 18

MOVING ON TO MADRID

Tottenham's Player of the Year was now in even higher demand. Luka still had five years left on his big new contract but that didn't stop other teams from trying to buy him. In 2010, it had been Manchester United; in 2011, it was Chelsea's turn. Their manager, Carlo Ancelotti, was looking for a new playmaker to one day take over from Frank Lampard.

'Modrić would be perfect,' the Italian told Chelsea's owner, Roman Abramovich. 'See if you can sign him.'

'£22million?' Daniel Levy laughed out loud when

he heard the offer. 'You've got to be joking!'

'Ok, how about £27million?' Abramovich asked, coming back with a second bid.

'No,' Tottenham's chairman replied with a shake of his head, 'that's still not enough!'

Luka did his best to ignore all the transfer talk but it wasn't easy. In recent years, Chelsea had won the Premier League title *and* two FA Cups. What had Luka won at Tottenham during that time? Nothing, not one single trophy!

'Come on, you can't leave now!' Gareth pleaded with him. 'We're getting better and better.'

On the final day of the transfer window, Chelsea came back with one last offer for Luka – £40million! That would make him one of the most expensive Premier League players ever, but...

'No,' Levy replied again, 'that's still not enough!'

'Oh well,' Luka said to himself. He was staying at Tottenham for at least one more year. No problem, he was a professional. He put the transfer talk behind him and got on with doing what he did best – playing fantastic football.

Early in the game against Liverpool, Gareth dribbled down the left wing and crossed it to Jermain Defoe. Jermain couldn't make the most of it but Luka could. He ran up and hit a right-foot rocket straight into the top corner.

Gooooooooooooooooooooaaaaaaaaaaaaaaaaallllllllllll llllllllllllllll!!!!!!!!!!!!!!!!!!!!

'Come on!' Luka roared up at the fans as he slid across the grass on his knees. It was the perfect way to show that he was still a Tottenham star.

Luka was just getting started. He set up Gareth's winner in the next game against Wigan with a curling corner-kick. *GOAL!*

A week later, he set up Kyle Walker's winning goal in the North London derby against Arsenal.

'We love you, Luka!' the fans cheered loudly.

However, it soon turned into another same old season:

Tottenham battled for the title but in the end, they finished fourth.

Tottenham did well in the FA Cup but in the end, they lost to Chelsea in the semi-finals.

Yet again, there was no trophy to show for all their hard work.

'We must be cursed!' Luka groaned.

After four years, he felt like he had reached his limit at Tottenham. Was it finally time for him to move on? He would always be grateful to the club for helping him to become a better player, but he needed a change and a new football challenge. At the age of twenty-six, he was ready to take another step forward and join one of the biggest clubs in the world, where he could win the top trophies.

'So, which clubs are interested in me?' Luka asked his agent.

Real Madrid would be a perfect fit. Their manager, José Mourinho, saw Luka as the midfield magician that they were missing.

Real already had attacking midfielders like Mesut Özil and Kaká.

Real already had defensive midfielders like Xabi Alonso and Sami Khedira.

But Luka was different; he was a proper central midfielder. He was someone who could do a bit of both, plus a whole lot more! He was clever, he was creative, and he was also a lot tougher than he looked.

'Let's make this transfer happen!' Luka urged his agent impatiently. 'What's taking so long?'

Just as the summer transfer window was about to close, the deal was finally done. Real made an offer of £30million and this time, Levy said yes. After a fond farewell to London, Luka was moving on to Madrid!

His first day as a Galáctico was one of the busiest and best days of his life. After passing his medical tests, Luka travelled to Real Madrid's Bernabeu Stadium. The club's president, Florentino Pérez, was there to greet him and hand him his brand-new white shirt. Xabi Alonso already wore the Number 14, so Luka went for 19 instead.

'Wow, this is really happening!' he thought to himself excitedly as they posed for photos together.

Once he was wearing the full Real Madrid kit, Luka ran proudly out onto the pitch with his wife, Vanja, and their young son, Ivano. As he looked around him, Luka couldn't stop smiling. This was their new home now. The stadium looked especially huge without the usual 80,000 supporters. It was certainly a lot bigger than that hotel car park in Croatia!

Luka's last job of the day was a press conference with all the Spanish journalists. He was Real's star signing of the summer, after all.

'I'm very happy and proud to be at the biggest and best club in the world,' Luka told them. 'I can't wait to get started!'

CHAPTER 19

FINDING HIS FEET IN MADRID

Just two days later, Luka made his Real Madrid debut in the Spanish Super Cup. With ten minutes to go, they were beating rivals Barcelona 2–1.

'Get ready!' a coach called out to him. 'You're coming on!'

Luka's heart was hammering in his chest. This was the big time now. He was about to play against Messi, Xavi and Iniesta, in front of 80,000 people!

To relax himself, Luka thought about what Bilić, the Croatia manager, had said to him, all those years ago: 'You can be one of the best midfielders in the world.'

Now, he had to prove it. Luka sat down next to

Mourinho on the bench and listened to his detailed instructions. The main one was simple, though: 'Don't lose the ball.'

No problem, he could definitely do that! As Luka high-fived Mesut and ran onto the field, Cristiano came over to talk to him. He had instructions of his own.

'Lots of nice, neat passes, okay?' the Portuguese superstar said. 'Come on, let's win this!'

At first, Luka kept things simple, but when he won the ball off Xavi, he rushed forward into the box. A goal on his Real Madrid debut? What a dream start that would be!

Cristiano passed to Karim Benzema, who pulled it back for Luka to... *NO, SHOT BLOCKED!*

'So close!' he groaned with his hands on his head.

Before he knew it, the match was over, and Real Madrid were the winners. On his third day at the club, Luka was already lifting his first trophy!

'Man, I love it here!' he laughed with Sergio Ramos as they carried the Super Cup around the stadium together.

'Just you wait,' the defender warned, 'our season is about to get a whole lot tougher!'

Luka's next big challenge was getting into the Real Madrid Starting XI. Yes, he had cost the club a lot of money, but he would have to earn his place. Xabi and Sami were Mourinho's first-choice midfielders, so that left Luka fighting for one space with Mesut.

For the first half of the season, they shared the role, but it was Mesut who started the big games, against Barcelona in La Liga and Borussia Dortmund in the Champions League. Luka, meanwhile, was struggling to impress. Twenty matches into his Madrid career, he only had one goal and one assist.

'I really need to do something special!' Luka told Vanja, his voice full of frustration. 'And soon!'

The Real fans didn't have much patience with new signings, especially new signings who cost £30million. They expected them to be superstars straight away. In December 2012, they voted Luka as the worst signing of the season.

'You've got to give Modrić more time,' Mourinho told the Spanish media. 'He's a very clever player but he's still getting used to playing for Real Madrid.'

The criticism hurt but Luka never stopped believing in himself. He was a lot stronger than he looked, both physically and mentally. How many times had people questioned his toughness? And how many times had he proved them wrong out on the football pitch? In Croatia, in Bosnia, in England... if Luka could do it there, then he could definitely do it in Spain too.

The turnaround began when Mourinho moved him back from attacking midfield to central midfield. That was the position where Luka felt most comfortable. That was where he had played his best games for Tottenham. That was where he would have the space to create his magic for Real Madrid.

Against Ajax in the Champions League, Luka won the ball with a brilliant sliding tackle, and then dribbled forward. What next? Cristiano was calling for it on the left, but there was Karim, making a brilliant run to the right. Luka found him with the perfect pass. Karim cut it back to Cristiano – *GOAL 1–0!*

'Great work, guys!' Cristiano cheered, high-fiving Karim and Luka.

Luka was really enjoying himself as Real's midfield maestro. *Control, spin, another perfect pass!* This time, it was José Callejón who ran in and scored. 2–0!

'You're on fire!' Sami shouted, giving Luka a big hug.

From that match onwards, it was clear what position he had to play. When Barcelona came to the Bernabeu, Luka started in central midfield. With ten minutes to go, he curled a corner-kick straight onto Sergio's head. *GOAL – 2–1 to Real Madrid!*

What a moment, what an atmosphere inside the stadium! Luka was the first to jump on Sergio, and the other players bundled on top. He really felt part of the team now.

Despite that important victory, Real Madrid wouldn't be able to catch Barcelona at the top of La Liga. However, they were still fighting for two other trophies: the Copa Del Rey and, Luka's favourite, the Champions League.

In the Round of 16, Real were losing 2–1 to Manchester United when Luka got the call from Mourinho. 'You're coming on!' Luka raced out onto the pitch at Old Trafford, ready to make an impact.

Control, turn, perfect pass!

Control, turn, perfect pass!

But when the space opened up on the edge of the United penalty area, Luka knew what to do:

Control, skip past the tackle, fire a swerving shot in off the post!

Goooooooooooooooooooaaaaaaaaaaaaaaaaaalllllllllllll lllllllllllll!!!!!!!!!!!!!!!!!!!

2–2! Luka punched the air with pride. He had only been on the field for six minutes! The Real Madrid fans had changed their minds. He was a hero now, and they chanted his name:

Modrić! Modrić! Modrić!

Real Madrid cruised past Galatasaray in the quarter-finals but they were destroyed by Robert Lewandowski's Dortmund in the semis.

Oh well, Luka still had one last trophy to play for. In the Copa Del Rey final, Real were up against their local rivals, Atlético Madrid.

Cristiano scored first with a powerful header but Diego Costa equalised for Atlético. Real attacked again and again, but somehow, they couldn't score a second goal. After ninety minutes, it was still 1–1 – and time for extra-time!

Luka was taken off and he watched from the bench as Atlético went on to win the final. No – another trophy lost! It was a sad end to his first season in Spain, but Luka had high hopes for his future at the club. After a difficult start, he was finding his feet in Madrid.

CHAPTER 20

TROPHY TIME AT LAST

There were lots of changes at Real Madrid during the summer of 2013. The previous season had been a failure; the team hadn't won one single major trophy! That just wasn't good enough for the biggest club in the world.

So, suddenly they had a new manager and top new players too. Fortunately, it was all good news for Luka. His new boss was Carlo Ancelotti, the man who had tried to sign him for Chelsea back in 2011. Phew, that meant that he was clearly a fan! And Real's new star signings included Luka's old Tottenham teammate, Gareth Bale.

'Hey, stop following me!' Luka joked but really

it was great to be reunited with his Welsh friend. Gareth was a very talented footballer and he shared the same ambition to lift lots of top trophies.

'We really should have won something together at Spurs,' Gareth admitted, 'but at least we've got another chance here!'

Real Madrid's top target for the 2013–14 season was winning the Champions League. They had won it nine times before in their history, but not since 2002. That was now over ten years ago.

'There's a curse on us,' some fans argued. 'We lost in the semi-finals for the last three years in a row!'

It was up to the Real Madrid players to prove that the curse didn't exist. It was up to them to go out there and win that difficult tenth trophy, '*La Décima*' as they called it in Spain.

As usual, they stormed through the group stage, winning five games out of six, and with scores like 6–1, 4–0, 4–1! Cristiano was having a field day, and even Luka scored one against FC Copenhagen. It was like his goal against Manchester United, only even better.

Touch, Cruyff turn away from the tackle, curling superstrike into the top corner!

Gooooooooooooooooooaaaaaaaaaaaaaaaaalllllllllllll llllllllllllll!!!!!!!!!!!!!!!!!!!!!

Even Cristiano was impressed. 'You've got real power in those little legs!' he said with a smile.

The Round of 16 was another stroll in the park: Real thrashed Schalke 9–2 on aggregate.

'Don't get carried away!' Ancelotti warned them as they celebrated. 'There are tougher tests ahead!'

Their manager was right. In the quarter-finals, they faced Borussia Dortmund, the team that had knocked them out the previous year.

'Right, time for revenge!' Cristiano announced with a focused look on his face.

Gareth poked a shot through the keeper's legs. *1–0!*

Isco shot low into the bottom corner. *2–0!*

At half-time, Real Madrid looked in total control. There was only one thing missing: a goal for Cristiano. Their superstar striker was desperate to score and Luka was happy to help him. That was part of his job as a midfield maestro.

Suddenly, Luka spotted a sloppy Dortmund pass and burst forward to intercept it. After a short dribble, he slipped a perfect pass through to Cristiano. *3–0!*

After doing his famous 'Superman' celebration, Cristiano hugged Luka tightly. 'You're the best!' he screamed joyfully.

Real Madrid were soon into the Champions League semi-finals for the fourth year in a row. Could they finally break the twelve-year curse and reach the final? To do that, they would need to beat Pep Guardiola's brilliant Bayern Munich.

But first, Real had another trophy to try and win. They reached the Copa Del Rey final once more, after taking sweet revenge on Atlético in the semi-finals with a 5–0 win.

Now, it was time for the ultimate *El Clásico* showdown: Real Madrid vs Barcelona. But The Whites would have to win it without their top goalscorer, Cristiano. He was injured for the big game.

'Come on, we can do this!' their captain Iker

Casillas called out before kick-off, clapping his gloves together. 'We're not a one-man team!'

No, they had so many superstars out on the pitch: Sergio and Pepe in defence; Luka and Xabi pulling the strings in midfield; and Gareth, Karim, Isco and Ángel in attack.

Real created chance after chance but they lacked that killer finish. Cristiano's killer finish. With fifteen minutes to go, the score was still 1–1.

Luka dribbled forward, past Sergio Busquets, and aimed for the bottom corner. His shot skipped up off the grass, past the diving keeper, but clipped the outside of the post.

'*Ohhhhhhhhhhhhhhhhhhhhh,*' the Madrid fans groaned in disappointment.

Luka stood there and stared at the goal in disbelief. How had his shot not gone in? Oh well, all they could do was keep trying...

Fábio Coentrão passed it down the line to Gareth, who flicked the ball around Marc Bartra and chased after it.

'Go on! Go on!' Luka urged his teammate on from

his own half. He had seen Gareth do it so many times for Tottenham.

Bartra had no chance of catching him. Gareth dribbled into the Barcelona box and nutmegged the keeper. *2–1!*

Luka punched the air but he knew that the match wasn't over yet. They had ten long minutes of defending to do. At last, the final whistle blew – Real Madrid were the winners!

'You did it – *we* did it!' Luka cheered, throwing his arm around Gareth's shoulder. Even after such an exhausting game, he was buzzing with excitement. 'TROPHY TIME!'

Instead of medals, the players each got a mini version of the Spanish Cup. Luka held onto his little trophy tightly throughout the night of celebrations.

Campeones, Campeones, Olé! Olé! Olé!

The next day, however, it was straight back to work.

'One down, one to go!' Ancelotti reminded his Real Madrid players at training.

The Copa Del Rey was just the delicious starter

before the Champions League main course. *Yummy!* Now that he had one trophy, Luka couldn't wait to win another.

Real Madrid had a clear plan for beating Bayern – defend well and then counter-attack at top speed. It worked perfectly.

'This is going to be our year!' Luka yelled at full-time. Real had just thrashed Bayern 4–0 in Germany. At last, they were in the Champions League final again!

Luka tried to keep as calm as possible but that wasn't easy. He was about to play the biggest match of his entire life – Real Madrid vs Atlético Madrid in the 2014 Champions League Final. He had dreamed of this moment ever since he first kicked a football.

As the two teams walked out of the tunnel, there was the trophy, gigantic and gleaming. Luka couldn't help taking one quick glance at it as he passed.

'I'll be lifting that later on!' he told himself confidently.

Luka got his wish, but only after an epic battle.

Atlético took the lead in the first half and they looked like they would hold on for victory.

But just when Real thought their Champions League dream was over, Luka curled in a dangerous corner-kick and Sergio scored an incredible header. 1–1!

'Yes!' Luka cheered, throwing his arms up in the air.

In extra-time, there was only going to be one winner.

Gareth headed in at the back post. *2–1!*

Marcelo hit a long-range strike. *3–1!*

Cristiano scored from the penalty spot. *4–1!*

Game over – Real Madrid were the new Champions of Europe!

Campeones, Campeones, Olé! Olé! Olé!

As his teammates sank to their knees on the pitch, Luka looked up at the sky. He was now a Champions League winner. It was a night that he would never forget. He just hoped that his beloved grandad was up there watching his proudest moment.

CHAPTER 21

2014: WORLD CUP DISAPPOINTMENT

Now that Luka was a European Champion at club level, could he go on and become a World Champion with his country? He hoped so, but it was going to be his biggest challenge yet.

After the excitement of Euro 2008, Croatia had lost their way. They hadn't even qualified for the 2010 World Cup, and at Euro 2012, they got knocked out in the group stage. Could the national team turn things around at the 2014 World Cup? The Croatian fans felt hopeful as they made the long trip to Brazil.

'Modrić, Rakitić, Mandžukić, Srna, Olić – this is our best squad since 1998!'

'Brazil will probably beat us, but we're better than Cameroon and Mexico!'

The Croatian players shared that hope. Their new coach was Niko Kovač, the legendary midfielder who had played alongside Luka at Euro 2008. He had put together a strong team with an exciting mix of raw talent and experienced leaders. Right-back Darijo Srna was the captain but at the age of twenty-eight, Luka was definitely Croatia's main man in the middle.

Luka was happy to take on that extra responsibility. After all, he was now used to handling the pressure of playing for Real Madrid. Plus, he would do anything to help his country. He had even had a smart new haircut for the special occasion!

When it came to World Cups, Luka had unfinished business. He had been waiting years for a second chance on the world stage. Back in 2006, he had been a young substitute; now, in 2014, he was a *Galáctico*, one of the best playmakers in the world.

'We've got to stick together tonight,' Luka told his midfield partner, Ivan Rakitić, as they prepared to take on Neymar Jr and co.

In front of 50,000 screaming Brazilians, Croatia took a surprise lead when Luka's club teammate Marcelo scored an own goal.

'Stay focused!' Darijo told his teammates.

Luka did his best to stop Neymar Jr, but eventually he found a little bit of space and scored.

'Keep going!' Kovač called from the sidelines.

Luka and his teammates showed real spirit. They battled on bravely but then Brazil were awarded a dodgy penalty.

'No way, that's a dive!' Luka argued angrily, but the referee had made up his mind.

What an annoying way to lose! Oh well – Croatia would still make it through to the second round as long as they beat Cameroon and Mexico. That seemed possible. The only problem was that Luka had picked up a foot injury.

'Don't worry, it's fine,' he reassured everyone as he hobbled down the tunnel. 'After a few days of rest, I'll be ready to go again!'

Luka knew that his country was counting on him. He couldn't let them down, especially not in a World

Cup! So, when Croatia kicked off against Cameroon, Luka was there in midfield with Ivan. Fortunately, he didn't need to be at his creative best, because his teammates took control.

Ivan Perišić crossed to Ivica. *1–0!*

Perišić sprinted through and scored himself. *2–0!*

Mario Mandžukić powered a header past the keeper. *3–0!*

Eduardo's shot was saved but Mario tapped home the rebound. *4–0!*

Croatia's World Cup campaign was totally back on track! Now, they just had to play with the same confidence against Mexico. Luka still wasn't fully fit, but he wasn't going to miss their biggest match in years. What if this turned out to be his last World Cup?

'Come on, let's show them how good Croatians can be!' Kovač cheered in the dressing room.

It was the ultimate showdown. Whichever nation won, would go through to the next round. After seventy-two tense minutes, it was Mexico who took the lead.

'Who was marking Márquez?' Luka groaned, throwing his arms up in frustration.

No, he had to stay strong and be a leader. Luka could see that heads were dropping, and he couldn't let that happen. Croatia needed him.

'Keep going, there's plenty of time left!' he urged his teammates on.

But when Luka led his team forward, Mexico hit them on the counter-attack: *2–0, then 3-0!* Perišić pulled a late goal back but it wasn't enough. Croatia were heading home.

Luka stood with his hands on his hips and let out a loud sigh. It was so disappointing. His head was full of 'if only's:

'If only we had scored the first goal!'

'If only the referee hadn't given that penalty to Brazil!'

'If only I hadn't got injured!'

But there was no point dwelling on the past. Their World Cup was over. The Croatian players had to pick themselves up and learn from their mistakes.

What Luka really needed was a rest. It had been

such a long, tough season, for both club and country. It was time for him to relax and unwind with his family and friends. Only after that would he be able to think about the next tournaments: Euro 2016 and the 2018 World Cup. By then, Luka would be thirty-two years old. It might well be his last chance to lead Croatia to glory.

CHAPTER 22

THE MIDFIELD MAESTRO OF MADRID

Luka hoped to get over his World Cup blues by winning lots more trophies with Real Madrid.

'Now that our Champions League curse is over, what's stopping us?' he argued.

But unfortunately, Real's next trophies didn't arrive until Zinedine Zidane took over as manager in 2016. With the slick Frenchman in charge, suddenly everything clicked into place. Every player's role was clear.

'You two will be my midfield maestros,' the new manager told Luka and Toni Kroos. 'You're the important link between defence and attack. Without you, we won't win a thing!'

Zidane wanted them to feel special and it worked. Luka and Toni's amazing midfield partnership helped Real Madrid to reach the quarter-finals, then the semi-finals, then the final of the Champions League.

'We're back where we belong!' Luka celebrated with Gareth after battling past Manchester City.

In the final, they were up against their Madrid rivals again. Atlético were looking for revenge; Real were looking for their eleventh title. '*La Undécima*' was now the aim.

This time, when he walked out of the tunnel, Luka didn't look at the big, shiny trophy in front of him. No, not even one little glance out of the corner of his eye! He had seen it before, and he had lifted it before. By the end of the night, he would make sure that he had it in his hands again.

'Let's do this!' Luka roared, feeling that now-familiar thrill.

However, the 2016 final turned out to be even tighter than 2014. On this occasion, it was Real who took the lead through Sergio, and Atlético who fought back. But when it came to extra-time, neither team could score. *Uh oh, time for penalties!*

Luka was willing to take one if he had to, but luckily, Real already had five stars from the spot. So instead, he watched from the halfway line with the rest of his anxious teammates, as...

Lucas Vázquez... SCORED!

Marcelo... SCORED!

Gareth... SCORED!

Sergio... SCORED!

Cristiano stepped up to win the shoot-out and... SCORED!

Real Madrid were the Champions of Europe once more! Luka jumped for joy and raced over to hug their hero, Cristiano.

Campeones, Campeones, Olé! Olé! Olé!

Would he ever grow tired of winning trophies? 'No, never!' Luka declared as the party started.

This time, Real were on a roll. They made it to the 2017 Champions League Final too, where they took on Juventus. They were on for the Quadruple! Real had already lifted the UEFA Super Cup, the FIFA Club World Cup, *and* the Spanish League title.

'If we win tonight, it's official,' Zidane told his players before kick-off. 'We'll be the greatest football team in the whole wide world!'

Luka loved the sound of that. That was why he had moved to Real Madrid in the first place – to play for the greatest football team in the world.

In his third Champions League Final, Luka was desperate to leave his mark on the match.

'This time, I want to score,' he told Sergio, 'or at least get another assist!'

Cristiano scored first, but then Luka's Croatian teammate, Mario, equalised with a wondergoal. 1–1. It was all to play for in the second half.

Real attacked again and again. Even Luka had a long-range shot but it was an easy save for a keeper like Gianluigi Buffon.

'No, what was that?' Luka groaned, kicking the air in anger.

When Juventus cleared the ball away, he chased back to get it. If Real kept the pressure up, eventually the goal would come.

But no, his midfield partner Casemiro was rushing

forward, ready to shoot. Luka got out of the way just in time. *BANG!* The ball deflected up off a defender and then dipped down into the bottom corner. *2–1 to Real Madrid!*

'Yes!' Luka screamed, throwing his arms up in the air.

What now – should Real sit back and defend their lead, or push forward for a third goal? The answer was simple; Luka always preferred to attack.

His energy levels were incredible. He raced over to the right wing to win the ball back and then kept on running. Dani Carvajal's pass looked like it would go out for a goal kick, but Luka stretched out his right leg and somehow kept it in. Not only that, but he managed to play a perfect cross to Cristiano. *3–1!*

Luka jumped back up to his feet in a flash. Yes, what a moment! He had another assist in a Champions League final. No, he wasn't a flashy goalscorer like Cristiano, but he was still just as important to the team. Where would Real Madrid be without their little midfield magician? Probably not winning back-to-back European titles!

'We're the greatest team in the whole wide world!' Luka cried out at the final whistle.

With a Croatia flag wrapped around his waist, he stood right next to Sergio as the captain collected the trophy and lifted it high into the sky.

'Hurray!' cheered the Real Madrid players, coaches and fans all together. They had just won the Quadruple! Luka now had a hat-trick of Champions League winners' medals. What was left for him to achieve?

'Lots!' he declared. Luka loved winning and he was always hungry for more. 'Right, let's win three in a row!'

That's exactly what Real Madrid did. On the way to yet another final, they beat Borussia Dortmund, PSG, Juventus *and* Bayern Munich. In the Champions League, they were simply unstoppable. With a team full of fighters like Sergio, Luka and Cristiano, no-one could knock them out!

Luka played almost every minute at the heart of the midfield. He was now the proud owner of the Real 'Number 10' shirt.

07 Cristiano, 08 Toni, 09 Karim, 10 Luka, 11 Gareth – what a dream team!

'You've really earned that!' Sergio laughed. 'Remember when you were "the worst signing of the season"?'

Of course Luka remembered. Like all criticism, it had motivated him to keep working hard and reach that next level.

In the 2018 Champions League Final, Real Madrid took on Liverpool. Before the game, everyone was talking about Sergio vs Mohamed Salah, and Cristiano vs Virgil van Dijk. But what about the big battle in midfield?

'That's where we'll win this match!' Luka told Toni and Casemiro confidently.

He was correct but the winning goals were very weird indeed. Either side of Gareth's brilliant bicycle kick, the poor Liverpool keeper made two massive howlers.

Firstly, Loris Karius tried to throw the ball out to Luka's Croatia teammate Dejan Lovren, but Karim blocked it and it rolled all the way into the net. *1–0!*

Secondly, Karius let Gareth's long-range shot slip straight through his gloves. *3–1!*

Real Madrid didn't mind; they were the Champions League winners for the third year in a row. For Luka and his teammates, it was becoming a regular thing.

'No big deal!' he joked with Marcelo, but it was a big deal.

Lisbon in 2014, Milan in 2016, Cardiff in 2017, Kiev in 2018 – Luka would never forget those four incredible European nights as a winner with Real.

CHAPTER 23

2018: WORLD CUP HOPE

For his club, Luka was the modest midfield maestro, launching attacks with neat, little passes. But his country expected more. They needed Luka to be their playmaker, goalscorer *and* matchwinner.

'No way, that's impossible for one player!' his friends defended him.

Sadly, Euro 2016 had been the same old story. Croatia started the tournament brilliantly but when Luka got injured, everything fell apart.

'Hey, it's not your fault,' Cristiano comforted him as he cried on the pitch after their defeat to Portugal. Luka felt like he'd let everyone down. 'Don't give up!'

No, Luka never gave up. Instead, he became the

new captain of Croatia. After over 100 international caps, he was ready to use his experience wisely. It was a huge honour, but also a huge responsibility, especially with a World Cup coming up. Every four years, the fans' excitement grew and grew, before ending in disappointment:

2006 – knocked out in the group stage,

2010 – didn't even qualify,

2014 – knocked out in the group stage.

That Mexico defeat still haunted Luka.

So, what could Croatia achieve in 2018? Whatever happened, Luka was determined to make his country proud in Russia. But he really believed that he could lead the team all the way to glory. Why not?

They certainly had enough talent in their squad. Dejan was their rock at the back and Mario was their target man up top. Then in between, they had Luka and Ivan Rakitić, two of the best midfielders in the world. At club level, they were rivals for Real Madrid and Barcelona, but for their country, they formed a perfect partnership.

'Luka and Iniesta are from a different planet,' Ivan

said admiringly. 'They are among the best players ever in their positions.'

Dejan, Luka, Ivan, Mario – people were calling them Croatia's second golden generation, twenty years on from the heroic days of Bilić, Boban and Šuker.

In order to succeed, the new Croatia team just needed to stay strong and not fall apart like before. Team spirit – that was what they needed to show. As the squad prepared for the tournament, Luka tried to relieve some of the pressure.

'Let's take one game at a time,' he told the players. 'Remember, our main target is to get past the group stage.'

In the first match against Nigeria, Luka led by example. He was Croatia's main man.

Control, turn, perfect pass,
Control, turn, perfect pass.

The captain's armband on his sleeve seemed to give him even more energy than usual.

It was Luka who took the corner that Peter Etebo flicked into his own net. *1–0!*

And it was Luka who took the penalty after Mario was fouled. *2–0!*

Gooooooooooooooooooooaaaaaaaaaaaaaaaaallllllllllll llllllllllllll!!!!!!!!!!!!!!!!!!!!!

'Yes!' he cheered, calmly punching the air as his teammates surrounded him.

Croatia were off to a perfect start, but next up were Argentina. That meant Sergio Agüero, Gonzalo Higuaín and Lionel Messi.

'You've got to work together tonight,' Croatia's manager Zlatko Dalić warned them before kick-off. 'If anyone switches off for a second, Messi will score!'

Ivan nodded. It was true; he trained with Lionel every day at Barcelona.

Argentina had lots of amazing attackers but in defence, they were all over the place. In the first-half, Perišić and Mario both missed glorious chances to score.

'Don't worry, just keep going!' Luka reassured his teammates.

Their captain's calmness spread. Early in the second half, the Argentina goalkeeper made a total

mess of his clearance. The ball bounced up in front of
Ante Rebić and he volleyed it in. *1-0!*

Luka joined in with the goal celebrations but he
knew that with Messi and Higuaín on the pitch,
Croatia would need more than one.

With ten minutes to go, Luka got the ball in acres
of space, just outside the penalty area. Danger alert
for Argentina!

Control, shift to the right, then right-foot rocket!

*Goooooooooooooooooooooaaaaaaaaaaaaaaaaallllllllllllll
lllllllllllllll!!!!!!!!!!!!!!!!!!!!!*

Luka raced away with both arms up in the air.
What a strike, and what an important time to score!
By the corner flag, Luka slid across the grass on his
knees. Soon, he was being squished in the middle of
a big squad hug.

In the last minute, Ivan made it 3–0. It was
a famous victory for Croatia, and it put them
through to the World Cup second round! Luka
couldn't stop smiling as he high-fived each of his
teammates. Finally, the national team was living up
to expectations.

'We did it – we're through!'

It was already Croatia's best World Cup performance since 1998. Suddenly, the team had to come up with new targets for the tournament. Quarter-finals? Semi-finals? FINAL?

'No, let's just take one game at a time,' Luka kept saying. They couldn't afford to get carried away.

With one group game still to play, surely it was time for Luka to have a well-deserved rest? In the knockout rounds, Croatia would need their classy captain to be at his magical best. But no, Luka wanted to play against Iceland.

'I'm fine, I can rest when the World Cup is over!' he decided. The most important thing for Croatia was to keep the momentum going.

So, Luka played the first sixty-five minutes in midfield, until his legs ached, and victory looked safe. Job done! He removed the armband and handed it to his best friend Vedran.

'Don't do anything stupid, okay?' Luka said with a cheeky smile.

'I'll try not to!' Vedran replied.

Then Luka trudged slowly off the pitch, with the Croatian fans chanting his name:

Modrić! Modrić! Modrić!

With three wins out of three, Croatia finished top of Group D. Luka's World Cup dream was alive and kicking.

CHAPTER 24

2018: WORLD CUP PRIDE AND JOY

In the Round of 16, the winner of Group D faced the runners-up in Group C. That meant Croatia vs Denmark.

'Nice, we'll definitely win that!' some players argued. 'They couldn't even beat Australia.'

Luka shook his head. No, no, no – they couldn't think like that! Confidence was good, but cockiness could end in disaster.

'It's a World Cup – anyone can beat anyone on their day! Just look at Germany – they lost to Mexico and South Korea. So, Denmark are dangerous, okay?'

A few hours before kick-off, some exciting news spread around the squad. Spain had just lost to the tournament hosts on penalties!

The route to the World Cup final was opening up beautifully for Croatia, thought Luka. They would face Russia in the quarter-finals, then England, Colombia, Sweden or Switzerland in the semis...

'No,' he stopped himself. 'We've got to take this one game at a time.'

But despite all their captain's warnings, Croatia got off to a dreadful start against Denmark. In the very first minute, Mathias Jørgensen scored, in an ugly goalmouth scramble. *1–0 to Denmark!*

Luka couldn't believe what he was watching. 'See!' he wanted to scream. 'Denmark *are* dangerous!'

Uh oh, were Croatia about to fall apart again? No, their team spirit was much stronger this time. Three minutes later, Mario made it 1–1.

'That's more like it!' Luka shouted, as he hugged the goalscoring hero.

It was an exciting, end-to-end match. Both teams had lots more chances to score but somehow, it was still 1–1 after ninety minutes.

Extra-time! When Ante dribbled around the

Denmark keeper, he looked certain to score the winning goal for Croatia. But Jørgensen slid in and fouled him before he could shoot. *Penalty!*

It was all up to Luka now. His entire country was counting on him. As he placed the ball down on the spot, he pictured it flying into the back of the net. It looked so easy in his head!

'Focus,' Luka muttered to himself. 'You have to be the hero.'

When the referee blew the whistle, he kicked it low and hard towards the bottom right corner… but Kasper Schmeichel had guessed the right way. *SAVED!*

Luka was devastated, but he didn't let it show. He had to stay strong for his team, his nation. He ran back and battled on until…

Penalty shoot-out! 'I'll take one,' Luka said straight away.

'Are you sure about this?' Dalić asked.

Luka just nodded. He was Croatia's captain and this was his chance to make up for the miss.

When it was his turn, Luka strode forward with

fire in his eyes. The two teams were tied at 1–1 in the shoot-out. If he missed again, it could be all over for Croatia. But if he scored… Yes, he had to think positively, like a leader. Should he go for the bottom right corner again, or switch to the top left instead? He wanted to keep the keeper guessing.

As Schmeichel dived, Luka aimed his penalty straight down the middle, just past his feet. *GOAL!*

'Yes!' Luka punched the air with passion and relief.

Suddenly, Croatia were on top. Their keeper Danijel Subašić made two super saves in a row. If Ivan scored, they won the shoot-out. Ivan stepped up and… SCORED!

When the ball crossed the goal line, Luka felt like his chest might explode. His penalty miss no longer mattered, because Croatia were through to the World Cup quarter-finals!

'Man, we don't make life easy for ourselves, do we?' Ivan and Luka laughed together.

The quarter-final against Russia turned out to be a nail-biter too. It was 1–1 at full-time and 2–2 after extra-time.

Time for another penalty shoot-out!

'Come on, one last push!' Luka went around telling his teammates. Although they were all absolutely exhausted, they managed to hold their nerve. Ivan scored the winning spot-kick again to send them into the semi-finals. The Croatian team collapsed in a big pile of sweaty bodies.

'Can you believe it, boys?' Mario cheered at the bottom. 'We're only one step away from the World Cup final!'

They clearly had the spirit, but did Croatia have enough energy to get there? After two marathon matches, Luka was running on empty, and the semi-final was only four days away.

Their opponents in that semi-final would be England. Gareth Southgate's team were playing with lots of confidence and their nation was right behind them. Everywhere the Croatia players went, the England fans were singing:

'It's coming home, it's coming home,
It's coming, FOOTBALL'S COMING HOME!'
'It's like they think they've beaten us already!'

160

Dejan snarled. 'Well, they haven't!'

That cocky song only made Croatia more motivated. Yes, they were tired, but they were about to play the biggest game of their lives. They simply *had* to win it.

'Even the guys in 1998 didn't get all the way to the final!' Dalić reminded them all. 'If you win tonight, you'll be national heroes forever!'

As Luka led his team out onto the pitch in Moscow, the atmosphere was amazing. The stands were a chequerboard of red and white. It felt, and sounded, like the whole of Croatia had come to Russia to cheer them on. There was nervous excitement everywhere. Could they do it? Could they *really* do it?

When Kieran Trippier curled an early free kick into Danijel's top corner, Croatia didn't panic. They had been 1–0 down before, against Denmark *and* Russia.

'We can turn this around!' Luka shouted. It was part of his job as captain, plus he had given away the free kick in the first place. He was determined to put things right.

The longer the game went on, the stronger they became. It was England, not Croatia, who looked like they'd played well over 500 minutes of football! Luka and Ivan were winning the midfield battle and pushing their team forward down the wings.

'Come on Croatia!' their fans roared. They could tell that a goal was coming...

Right-back Šime Vrsaljko delivered a dangerous cross and Perišić flicked it in. 1–1!

As the Croatian players celebrated together, Dejan shouted out, 'We can go on and win this now!'

They had to wait until the 109th minute, but Luka never stopped believing. One goal, and Croatia would be in the World Cup final. At last, Perišić headed the ball on to Mario and he shot past Jordan Pickford. 2–1!

At the final whistle, there were emotional scenes all over the pitch. Luka hugged Mario so tightly that they fell to the floor together.

'We did it! We did it!' they cheered again and again.

No matter what happened in the final against

France, Luka's Croatia team had made history. What an achievement! It was hard to describe the pride that the players all felt. They were the heroes who had put their country on the football map again.

But Luka wasn't settling for second place. No way! As Croatia's captain, he wanted to lift the trophy, the most famous trophy of all.

'Without doubt, winning the World Cup would be the greatest success of my career,' he told FIFA TV.

Sadly, it wasn't to be. In the final, France were just too strong for Croatia. It was only 2–1 at half-time but midway through the second half, Paul Pogba and Kylian Mbappé scored two quick goals. Game over.

At the final whistle, Luka walked around the pitch with his hands on his head and tears in his eyes. He had given absolutely everything for Croatia but in the end, it wasn't quite enough.

'We came so close!' he moaned to himself.

Despite the heartbreak, Luka still shook hands with all the France players. He also went up to collect a very special award: the Golden Ball, the prize for the World Cup's Best Player.

In the photos with Mbappé, the Best Young Player, Luka was too upset to smile. How could he? The trophy he was holding wasn't the trophy that he really wanted.

Luka was the ultimate team player, but in the months to come, he picked up two more prestigious prizes of his own. First, he won the Best FIFA Men's Player award and then the biggest of them all:

'The Ballon d'Or goes to... LUKA MODRIC!'

Wow, for the first time in eleven years, the winner wasn't Cristiano Ronaldo or Lionel Messi. For Luka, it was an unbelievable feeling.

'Thank you, 2018 has been a dream year for me,' Luka told the audience of top football people.

But it wasn't just that year – his whole career was a dream come true. From kicking a ball outside the Hotel Kolovare in Zadar, Luka had battled all the way to greatness. Too small, too weak? No way! He had risen to every challenge, in Croatia, Bosnia, England *and* Spain.

Luka had shown the strength to succeed, as well as the amazing midfield magic. He was a four-time

Champions League winner, a World Cup finalist, and now, officially the best footballer in the whole wide world.

LUKA MODRIĆ HONOURS

Dinamo Zagreb

🏆 Croatian First League: 2005–06, 2006–07, 2007–08

🏆 Croatian Super Cup: 2006

🏆 Croatian Cup: 2006–07, 2007–08

Real Madrid

🏆 Spanish Super Cup: 2012, 2017

🏆 Copa Del Rey: 2013–14

🏆 UEFA Champions League: 2013–14, 2015–16, 2016–17, 2017–18

🏆 UEFA Super Cup: 2014, 2016, 2017

🏆 FIFA Club World Cup: 2014, 2016, 2017

🏆 Liga: 2016–17

France U19
🏆 UEFA European Under-19 Championship: 2016

Individual
🏆 Bosnian Premier League Player of the Year: 2003

🏆 Croatian Football Hope of the Year: 2004

🏆 Prva HNL Player of the Year: 2007

🏆 Croatian Footballer of the Year: 2007, 2008, 2011, 2014, 2016, 2017

🏆 UEFA Euro Team of the Tournament: 2008

🏆 Tottenham Hotspur Player of the Year: 2010–11

🏆 UEFA Champions League Team of the Season: 2013–14, 2015–16, 2016–17, 2017–18

🏆 La Liga's Best Midfielder: 2013–14, 2015–16

🏆 FIFA World Cup Golden Ball: 2018

🏆 FIFA World Cup Dream Team: 2018

🏆 The Best FIFA Men's Player: 2018

🏆 Ballon d'Or: 2018

MODRIC

(10) THE FACTS

NAME: LUKA MODRIĆ

DATE OF BIRTH:
9 September 1985

AGE: 33

PLACE OF BIRTH:
Zadar

NATIONALITY: Croatian

BEST FRIEND:
Vedran Ćorluka

CURRENT CLUB: Real Madrid

POSITION: CM

THE STATS

Height (cm):	172
Club appearances:	603
Club goals:	74
Club trophies:	20
International appearances:	118
International goals:	14
International trophies:	0
Ballon d'Ors:	1

★ ★ ★ **HERO RATING: 88** ★ ★ ★

GREATEST MOMENTS

Type and search the web links to see the magic for yourself!

1 21 APRIL 2007, KAMEN INGRAD 0–1 DINAMO ZAGREB

https://www.youtube.com/watch?v=PCOKvQyRmoA
In only his second season at Dinamo, Luka led his team to the Croatian Treble. Most of the time, he was the clever little playmaker, setting up goals for his strike partner, Eduardo. But when they needed him, Luka stepped up and scored himself. This dipping half-volley was the goal that won Dinamo the league title.

169

2 12 JUNE 2008, CROATIA 2–1 GERMANY

https://www.youtube.com/watch?v=J_UACNCLYİM

Euro 2008 was a big breakthrough for Luka.
He scored the winner in Croatia's first game
against Austria, and then produced a real midfield
masterclass against Germany. Luka was the classiest
player on the pitch and he pushed his team forward
to a famous victory. Suddenly, Tottenham fans were
super-excited about their new signing...

3 21 MARCH 2009, TOTTENHAM 1–0 CHELSEA

https://www.youtube.com/watch?v=e-RDcB8KME8

Luka struggled at the start of his Premier League
career, but this was the match where he found his
best form. Whenever he got the ball, it was like
he had all the time in the world. Chelsea had no
chance. Luka passed, he dribbled, and he even
scored the winning goal! Soon, he would be one of
the top playmakers in the world.

★ 4 24 MAY 2014, REAL MADRID 4–1 ATLÉTICO MADRID (AFTER EXTRA-TIME!)

https://www.youtube.com/watch?v=IuIHU1lrvSQ

With seconds to go, it looked like Luka was about to lose his first Champions League final. But from his curling corner kick, Sergio Ramos scored a header, and the rest is history! Real Madrid have now won four European trophies with Luka in the team. His midfield magic is so important to the team.

★ 5 21 JUNE 2018, ARGENTINA 0–3 CROATIA

https://www.youtube.com/watch?v=m5QhsHXKQik

Luka was wonderful throughout the 2018 World Cup, but this was probably his best performance. Messi and Argentina were no match for Croatia's little midfield maestro. He controlled the game and even scored a right-foot rocket. With Luka wearing the captain's armband, his country was on its way to the World Cup Final!

PLAY LIKE YOUR HEROES

THE LUKA MODRIĆ
LONG-RANGE ROCKET

SEE IT HERE You Tube

https://www.youtube.com/watch?v=XVjV1T-U3jA&t=31s

STEP 1: Be patient! You're a midfield magician, not a striker. But when that space opens up…

Step 2: Get your position right! If you're not in the right place, how are you going to score? Wait around the edge of the penalty area…

Step 3: Make sure your first touch is good! You want to make a little room to strike the ball.

Step 4: As a defender rushes you, beat them with skill – a stepover or a Cruyff turn!

Step 5: When the gap opens up, it's time to go for goal. If the box is crowded, you might need to curl the ball around players. Whatever you do, aim for the corner of the net.

Step 6: GOAL! You're not a show-off like Cristiano Ronaldo, so a big smile will do for a celebration!

TEST YOUR KNOWLEDGE

1. What was the name of the hotel where Luka first started kicking a football?

2. Who was pictured on Luka's first pair of shin pads?

3. Which Croatian club rejected Luka when he was ten years old?

4. What funny exercise did Luka do to try and grow taller?

5. Who were Luka's three heroes from the Croatian team of Euro 96 and World Cup 98?

6. Luka formed a deadly duo at Dinamo with which striker?

7. How much did Tottenham pay for Luka in 2008?

8. How much did Real Madrid pay for Luka in 2013?

9. Gareth Bale followed Luka from Tottenham to Real Madrid – true or false?

10. How many Champions League Final assists does Luka have?

11. How many goals did Luka score at the 2018 World Cup (including penalty shoot-outs!)?

Answers below. . . No cheating!

1. The Hotel Kolovare 2. The Brazilian striker Ronaldo 3. His favourite team, Hajduk Split 4. He used to hang from the crossbar by his arms to stretch them! 5. Slaven Bilić, Zvonimir Boban and Davor Šuker 6. Eduardo 7. £16million 8. £30million 9. True – Gareth moved to Madrid one year after Luka 10. Two – one for Sergio Ramos in 2014 and one for Cristiano Ronaldo in 2017 11. Four (including two in penalty shoot-outs!)

HAVE YOU GOT THEM ALL?

FOOTBALL HEROES

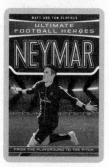